American Catholics

American Catholics

Gender, Generation, and Commitment

WILLIAM V. D'ANTONIO
JAMES D. DAVIDSON
DEAN R. HOGE
KATHERINE MEYER

ALTAMIRA
PRESS

A Division of
ROWMAN & LITTLEFIELD PUBLISHERS, INC.
Walnut Creek • Lanham • New York • Oxford

ALTAMIRA PRESS
A Division of Rowman & Littlefield Publishers, Inc.
1630 North Main Street, #367
Walnut Creek, CA 94596
www.altamirapress.com

Rowman & Littlefield Publishers, Inc.
4720 Boston Way
Lanham, MD 20706

12 Hid's Copse Road
Cumnor Hill, Oxford OX2 9JJ, England

British Library Cataloging in Publication Information Available

Library of Congress Cataloging-in-Publishing Data
American Catholics: gender, generation, and commitment / William V. D'Antonio . . . [et al.].
    p. cm.
    Includes bibliographical references and index.
    ISBN 0-7591-0040-3 (cloth : alk. paper)—ISBN 0-7591-0041-1 (pbk. : alk. paper)
    1. Catholic Church—United States. 2. United States—Church history. I. D'Antonio, William V.

BX1406.2. .A645 2001
282'.73'090511—dc21   2001022048

Printed in the United States of America

Contents

Foreword

Today's leader in the Church considers five sources of guidance when making decisions: (1) divine revelation (Sacred Scripture and Tradition); (2) the history of the Church (universal and particular) and the development of Catholic teaching and life; (3) prayer and reflection; (4) contemporary research about people (their interests, beliefs, values, and concerns) and their reception of the teachings of the Church; and (5) personal intuition and inspiration. All of these sources are of value and deserve attention and use in the process of leadership. Admittedly, not all come into play for every decision a leader has to make on a given day. They serve, rather, as a backdrop—a remote preparation, if you will—for the deliberations needed. Together they form a way of thinking and acting in the making of decisions.

A presupposition of such leadership is that God is at work in history, revealing the divine plan, and that Christians of every age have an obligation to understand the signs of the times and follow their lead. There is also a continuing need in the Church for discernment in the matter of doctrine and morals, a task that has been assigned to the teaching office of the Church. Since the Second Vatican Council, there has begun the practice of communal discernment done through prayer, dialogue, and honest exchange of viewpoints.

Following the Second Vatican Council, there has also been an emphasis on the study of culture and how the Gospel can be inculturated into the thinking and the lives of people and thus transform the culture. In fact, our Holy Father, Pope John Paul II, established a special council in this matter, the Pontifical Council for Culture. In one of his recent encyclical letters, *Fides et Ratio,* the Holy Father once again gave serious attention to the interaction of faith and reason. A number of postconciliar synodal documents and church teachings have reflected the spirit of *Gaudium et Spes,* teaching that "In pastoral care, sufficient use must be made not only of theological principles, but also the findings of the secular sciences, especially psychology and sociology, so that the faithful may be brought to a more accurate and mature life of faith" (N.62).

Pastoral leaders often are inclined, however, to attach little value to the findings of such secular sciences. I well remember an occasion when I was presenting a workshop to priests of a particular diocese. We were considering the various processes involved in pastoral planning. One of the priests participating in the workshop observed, "Why go through all of this? The Holy Spirit simply tells me what is to be done. I then announce it to the parishioners. They, then, are to obey." Such an exclusive inspiration misses the value of harvesting what the Holy Spirit reveals in the gathered Community, testing it, and harvesting what is received.

At times, pastoral leaders are tempted to rely on their own past theological formation, and they neglect to learn where the parishioners are on various topics and how they receive that which God is offering through the Church in a particular circumstance. Or they put a personal twist on an issue through reliance on their own understanding, interpretation, or opinion, causing some persons to reject what is offered.

Research in which believers share what they have discerned enhances the wisdom church leaders acquire through the pursuit of truth in other ways. Sharing the results of a research study upon its completion offers the further opportunity to refine and test current wisdom. Revelation can be considered in light of the existential, resulting in deeper personal meaning.

Researchers follow a professionally developed process in the search for the truth about a given topic. There are checks and balances, both internal and external, that evaluate the quality of method and the veracity of what has been discovered. Peer critique in professional forums and journals further assesses the quality of any study.

Research that is most helpful to pastoral leaders is the kind known as client-oriented applied research, not theoretical research of a more remote nature. While the latter is helpful in the construction of theories and new ideas, pastoral leaders are aided more often by research that speaks to the needs of a particular time or situation.

An interesting phenomenon associated with being a researcher is the experience of being slain for any bad news one brings to the table following a study. Unfortunately, one who brings unexpected or less-than-desired findings about what is happening in the Church sometimes is accused of being disloyal or unfaithful to the Church. Motivation will be questioned, methods used will be discounted, and interpretations of the data (statistical or otherwise) will be rejected when reports of the research findings do not support the assumption or hypotheses of people with different viewpoints. This aspect of doing research constitutes an occupational hazard, particularly in the Church. Perhaps this is why so many eminently qualified young researchers refrain from applying their professional skills in connection with the Church. Church leaders sometimes give no financial priority to research, either, and are happy to function without it. A question remains, however: Can today's pastoral leader function effectively without the contributions that scientific research can offer?

Given the dangers of engaging in research for the Church, one can appreciate all the more the work of those who embark on such a journey. The authors of this work have served the Church well for many years. In this book they share many insights that will be helpful to church leaders.

In this book we witness a reflection on how pastoral decision making can be assisted. The authors—William V. D'Antonio, James Davidson, Dean R. Hoge, and Katherine Meyer—present nine chapters of information and reflection about trends and issues in Catholicism in America, Catholic identity, religious practices, moral authority and praxis, Catholic social teaching, ministry, and participation of the faithful. The information they offer to us comes out of studies over twelve years and refers to other significant research findings. Suggestions are made for pastoral action in response to some of the research findings, particularly in the last chapter. Issues pertaining to race and ethnicity among Catholics are reported in an appendix.

The reader of this book will have a lot to consider. Fortunately, most of what one reads has to do with the faithful, what they note and do in the Church, and how they see themselves as a significant part of the Church. It is in Jesus Christ, with the guidance of the Holy Spirit, that all of us come together in knowing the truth and in offering our prayers of thanksgiving and worship to God, our Father and Creator.

May this work serve well the Lord and all of those who read it.

William B. Friend, D.D.
Bishop of Shreveport

Acknowledgments

We are grateful for the support and assistance of many organizations and individuals. This book is the third in a series of studies of Catholic laity, the first two of which were supported by the *National Catholic Reporter*. *NCR* also helped publicize the 1999 survey by publishing an attractive ten-page supplement depicting our findings (October 29, 1999). The publisher and editor, Tom Fox and Tom Roberts, provided help and advice. The Louisville Institute provided a grant to support the 1999 survey, and we thank Dr. James Lewis, the executive director, for his encouragement and support, enabling us to continue our study of Catholic trends.

During the research process we were helped by Harry Cotugno of the Gallup Organization and several research assistants: Xiaoyan Wang, Yingli Hao, Ann Kasprzyk, Mary Anne Eley, Brian Brown, Peter Veracka, and Frank DeRego. We were given helpful advice on earlier drafts by David O'Brien and Beverly McPherson, and a total review of the manuscript by Betty Seaver. Edward McCarthy prepared the index. We thank the editors of AltaMira Press, Mitch Allen, Erik Hanson, and Dorothy Bradley for their enthusiastic support and their commitment to sociological research on religion. We thank the Most Reverend Bishop William Friend for writing a foreword emphasizing the importance of this research to the Catholic community.

Finally we thank our families for their patience and forbearance during the year we labored on this project.

Chapter One

Setting the Stage: Trends and Issues in Catholicism in America

Here's the scene. It's 1900. There are about 12 million American Catholics and the number is growing every day, mainly because of European immigration. A predominantly Irish clergy and a multiethnic laity face many challenges, including a multiplicity of languages and a pressing need for churches and schools. Though the challenges seem insurmountable, this also is a period of great hope for the future.

A bishop and the priests of his diocese are meeting at the chancery. They are discussing the future, wondering what will happen in the Catholic Church during the next hundred years. They correctly project that the Catholic population will continue to grow. They also are right in predicting that, over time, Catholics will work their way up to the middle class. But there is no way on earth they would have predicted many of the other changes that have taken place during the past hundred years. They would never have foreseen the Second Vatican Council. Or that one day the Mass would be conducted in English. Or that Catholics would be attending Bible study. How could they ever have predicted the declining number of priests and sisters, or the growing number of lay ministers working in parishes and dioceses? They certainly would not have imagined nuns wearing street clothes, Catholics talking about their church as if it were "just another denomination," or "altar boys" who are girls. Nobody in the group would ever have guessed that by the end of the century, about one-third of the students at many Protestant colleges and universities would be Catholic. Even the bishop probably could never have pictured himself and his fellow bishops consulting with economists and social scientists as they prepared a pastoral letter on economic justice in the 1980s. Or the day when Catholics, making up 23 percent of the U.S. population, would be 29 percent of the U.S. House of Representatives and 23 percent of the U.S. Senate.

1

Our point is this: The twentieth century has been a time of incredible changes in the Catholic Church. Some have involved the status of Catholics in American society. Others are related to the norms and values in the Church itself. Together, these societal and organizational changes have raised important questions about what it means to be Catholic in the United States today.

This chapter describes the improving status of American Catholics and the changes that have taken place in the Church during the past century. Once we have established the current social and religious context, we identify a series of questions that American Catholics are asking as they enter the twenty-first century.

THE CHANGING STATUS OF AMERICAN CATHOLICS

The past hundred years have wrought a transformation in the status of American Catholics. The number of Catholics has grown steadily, and Catholics have moved up the social ladder. They also have moved from the margins to the middle of society, out of the so-called Catholic ghetto into a more ecumenical world. Finally, as European immigration has slowed and immigration from Asia, Latin America, and South America has increased, Catholics in the United States are gradually becoming a people of many colors. These trends are summarized in table 1.1 and described in the text that follows.

From Small to Large

Catholics always have been a numerical minority in the United States. There were roughly 40,000 Catholics in the colonies at the time the U.S. Constitution was ratified; by 1836, about 650,000. With large-scale immigration from Europe during the nineteenth century, the number had soared to 9 million in 1890 (about 14 percent of the total population).

As the twentieth century began, 12 million Catholics constituted 16 percent of the population (see table 1.2) Shaughnessy ([1925] 1969) and continued to increase rapidly until the Immigration Act of 1924 curtailed immigration as a whole, and especially immigration from predominantly Catholic countries. By then, there were more than 20 million Catholics in this country (about 19 percent of the total population). With only a trickle of new Catholic immigrants between the 1930s and 1960s, the Catholic population grew more slowly. By mid-century, the Catholic population was 29 million but remained at 19 percent of the whole. Since then, it has expanded briskly, principally as a result of the post–World War II baby boom and a new wave of immigration. Puerto

Table 1.1. Trends in Twentieth-Century Catholicism

	1900–1930s	1940s–1960s	1970s–2000
Catholics as percentage of U.S. population	~ 18%	~ 20%	~ 23%
Socioeconomic status	Lower	Lower middle	Upper middle
Prejudice and discrimination	Severe	Moderate	Limited
Catholics' social relations	Highly segregated	Somewhat segregated	Highly integrated
Race and ethnicity	White European	White European	Increasingly diverse
Meaning of "Church"	Institution	In transition	People of God
Locus of moral authority	External (magisterium)	In transition	Internal (conscience)
Authority in the Church	Highly centralized	In transition	More collegial
Church leaders	Male clergy	Male clergy	More lay ministers, women
Concept of God	Punitive	In transition	Loving
Liturgy	Uniform, laity is passive	In transition	Variable, laity is active
Relation between Church and world	Segregated	In transition	Integrated
Church's view of other faiths	Differences stressed	In transition	Similarities emphasized

Rican arrivals in the 1950s augmented the Catholic population (Fitzpatrick 1971) such that by 1960, it was approximately 42 million (about 23 percent of the total population). In 1965, President Lyndon Johnson lifted the lid on immigration, ushering in a wave of newcomers mostly from Central and South America and Asia, the majority of whom were Catholic (Christiano 1991). As a result, the Catholic population rose from 48 million in 1970 to 62 million in 1999 (*Official Catholic Directory* 2000). As we enter the new millennium, about one-quarter of the U.S. population is Catholic, about half is Protestant, and the remainder belongs to other religions or claims no religious affiliation.

From Poverty to Prosperity

Most eighteenth- and nineteenth-century Catholic immigrants came with limited educational backgrounds and took low-status, low-wage jobs (Dolan 1985; D'Antonio et al. 1996). By any measure of social and economic status, most Catholics were poor or nearly poor. With the passage of time and a great

Table 1.2. U.S. Catholic Population: 1900–99

Year	Millions of Catholics	Percentage of U.S. Population
1900	12	16
1910	16	17
1920	20	19
1930	20	16
1940	22	17
1950	29	19
1960	42	23
1970	48	24
1980	50	23
1990	59	23
1999	62	23

Sources: Data from Gerald Shaughnessy, *Has the Immigrant Kept the Faith?* (New York: Arno Press and The New York Times, [1925] 1969); *Official Catholic Directory,* annual eds. (New Providence, N.J.: P. J. Kenedy.)

deal of effort, they climbed up the socioeconomic ladder, achieving parity with Protestants by mid-century (Glenn and Hyland 1967; Greeley 1977). Though Catholics still lagged behind elite Protestants, such as Episcopalians, Presbyterians, and members of the United Church of Christ, they ranked ahead of evangelical groups, such as the Nazarenes and Baptists, and were more or less equal in status with Methodists and Lutherans (Roof and McKinney 1987).

Even while absorbing a new wave of Asian and Latino immigrants, Catholics continued their upward social mobility. A 1995 national study (Davidson et al. 1997) shows that of all Catholics who have completed their schooling, 29 percent are college graduates, have gone on to postgraduate work, or have completed graduate or professional degrees. Two-thirds of Catholics are white-collar workers (35 percent are executives, managers, or professionals). Forty percent have family incomes of $50,000 or more. Catholics are now well above the national average in educational achievement, occupational status, and family income. Still a bit behind the most elite Protestant groups, they are among the nation's most prosperous religious groups (Davidson, Pyle, and Reyes 1995).

From the Margins to the Middle

At the beginning of the twentieth century, Catholics lived on the margins of American society. The predominantly Protestant population tended to view the United States as a Protestant nation. Catholics were intruders who, it was said, threatened to contaminate the white, Anglo-Saxon, Protestant culture. Catholics were seen as mindless followers of the pope ("papists") and idolatrous believers in a misguided faith that stressed saints and statues (e.g., the Blessed Virgin Mary, Our Lady of Guadalupe) instead of the scriptures. As Al Smith's unsuccessful 1928 bid to become the first Catholic president indicated, the Church was seen as a hierarchical and authoritarian threat to the country's democratic ethos. Smith was accused in the campaign of being a papist who, if elected, might make the pope a member of his cabinet and force the nation to follow Roman ways (Moore 1956). Anti-Catholic organizations such as the Ku Klux Klan promulgated patently untrue stories about the sexual lives of Catholic priests and sisters. Newspaper cartoons and hate literature spread stereotypes of Irish Catholics as drunken fighters and Italian Catholics as members of the Mafia. Parish buildings and convents were burned. Catholic priests, sisters, and laypeople were attacked and killed. Catholics were denied jobs on the basis of their religion (Dolan 1985; Morris 1997; Gillis 1999).

Despite these obstacles, Catholics gradually moved into the middle class, assimilated into the American way of life, and modified some of their religious practices. As these changes took place, the nation began to be more accepting of Catholics. The number of Catholics on the faculties of leading colleges and universities increased (Steinberg 1974). The intelligence of high-profile Catholics such as William Buckley, Daniel Patrick Moynihan, Thomas Merton, Garry Wills, and John Noonan was widely recognized (Allitt 1993). Together, these developments fostered a new perception of Catholics as literate and cultured people. As Catholics enlisted in military service, fought bravely in World Wars I and II, and vigorously opposed "godless communism" during the Cold War era, the perception of Catholics as strangers and threats to American life waned. As the Church abandoned Latin for English, eliminated the "fish-on-Friday" rule, and toned down its emphasis on Mary, the Protestant majority found Catholics more acceptable members of the Christian tradition. Thirty-two years after Al Smith's failed attempt at the presidency, John F. Kennedy's election as the nation's first Catholic president was a sign that the Catholics were becoming full-fledged members of the society.

As we have seen in the recent controversy over not selecting a Catholic chaplain for the U.S. House of Representatives (Shields 1999); in Bob Jones University's assertions that the Catholic Church is a "satanic cult" and the pope is the "anti-Christ" (Martin 2000); and in continuing media bias against the Church (Lockwood 1999), anti-Catholicism is a lingering presence. Yet anti-Catholicism is nowhere near as virulent or widespread as it was at the outset of the twentieth century. Catholics, especially young Catholics, no longer live in fear of being singled out and discriminated against solely on the basis of their religion. They consider themselves fully American and tend to be perceived in the same way.

From Segregation to Integration

In the early decades of the 1900s, many Catholics lived in what can be called a Catholic ghetto that included parishes, parochial grade schools, Catholic high schools, Catholic hospitals, Catholic convents, Catholic newspapers, Catholic sororities and fraternities, even Catholic professional associations (Cogley and Van Allen 1986; Herberg, 1960). It was a total community headed by priests and sisters, a self-contained society whose religious leaders were fully supported by Catholic families.

Young Catholics were warned not to venture beyond the ghetto, for fear that they might come into contact with the wrong types of people (non-Catholics) and might lose their faith. Confined to the ghetto, they got their faith and morals from one place: the Church. What they learned in their catechism and parochial school classes (most of which were taught by priests and sisters) was reinforced not only by their parents but also by their grandparents, aunts, uncles, coaches, and Boy Scout or Girl Scout troop leaders.

The ghetto persisted into the 1940s and 1950s, when its walls began to crumble. With the end of World War II, the passage of the G.I. Bill increased access to higher education and inaugurated unprecedented rates of upward social mobility. Catholics moved out of older, inner-city neighborhoods into new suburbs, where they often lived side by side with Protestants and Jews. Their sons and daughters sought admission to Catholic colleges and universities, but also to state-supported colleges and universities and even elite Protestant schools. Meanwhile, in the ecumenical spirit of Vatican II, many specifically Catholic organizations (e.g., Catholic Boy Scouts and Catholic Girl Scouts) disbanded in favor of having Catholics participate in comparable communitywide organizations.

As the walls dividing the Catholic and non-Catholic worlds tumbled, young Catholics were increasingly exposed to the spiritual and moral ideas of non-Catholics in non-Catholic settings. Grade-school- and high-school-age Catholics read the Bible and said the Protestant version of the "Our Father" in public schools. Catholic students enrolled in secular and predominantly Protestant colleges and universities, where they took philosophy and sometimes theology courses from professors of other faiths and instructors with no religious preference. Catholic students in these settings also interacted with, and sometimes married, students who were not Catholic. As a result, they learned about faith and morals from many sources, not just the Church.

From White Europeans to People of Color

Before 1924, Catholic immigrants to this country came mainly from Europe. For example, in 1900 more immigrants were from Italy than any other single nation. The Immigration Act of 1924 curtailed immigration of all kinds, especially from predominantly Catholic countries in eastern and southern Europe. Though immigration was reduced from a flood to a trickle between 1924 and 1965, the vast majority of Catholics entering this country in the 1940s and 1950s were white Europeans (Dolan 1985; Christiano 1991). Well into the 1980s and early 1990s, more than 80 percent of all U.S. Catholics were white Europeans (D'Antonio et al. 1989; Davidson et al. 1997).

In 1965, the immigration laws were changed. According to the U.S. Bureau of the Census (*Statistical Abstracts of the United States* 1999, 11), between 1981 and 1996 immigrants came mainly from Mexico (3.3 million), the Philippines (844,000), Vietnam (719,000), China 657,000), India (498,000), Korea (453,000), El Salvador (362,000), Jamaica (323,000), and Haiti (255,000). A majority of those immigrants were Catholic (Christiano 1991, 173). As a consequence, the percentage of white Europeans in American Catholicism is declining and the percentage of non-Europeans and people of color is growing. Davidson's 1995 national survey showed that 89 percent of U.S. Catholics born in or before 1940 are white, and 72 percent of those born since 1961 are white. Only 7 percent of older Catholics are Latinos, compared with 20 percent of younger Catholics. Froehle and Gautier (2000) show that the racial composition of American Catholics continues to change.

CHANGES IN THE CHURCH

The Catholic Church includes everyone who follows Christ in the Catholic tradition. Most Catholics are laypeople. Others, including brothers, sisters, and monks, are called to life in religious communities. Still others—such as the pope, cardinals, bishops, priests, and deacons—are called to ordained life. Once they have received proper theological and spiritual training, the ordained are allowed to perform sacramental and other functions that laypeople cannot perform.

Like all large organizations, the Church has developed a set of offices or leadership positions that have special responsibilities for carrying out functions that "aim at the common good of the whole body" (Flannery 1992, 369). These offices and all the people who occupy them make up the "hierarchy." Office holders who have particular responsibility for maintaining and professing Catholic doctrine (the pope, cardinals, and bishops) are known as the "magisterium." The hierarchy and the magisterium play a major role in formulating, preserving, and reformulating Church norms and values.

Many of the norms and values of the Church remained quite stable during the twentieth century. The most stable of all are embedded in the Nicene Creed (which Catholics repeat at each Mass) and authoritative Church documents such as the *Catechism of the Catholic Church* (1995). For example, the Church consistently has taught that there are three persons in one God; that Jesus was divine yet fully human; that Jesus died for our sins and rose again from the dead; that Mary is the Mother of God; and that in the sacrament of the Eucharist, the bread and wine are transformed into the Body and Blood of Christ. These beliefs are as much the bedrock of Catholic teaching today as when they were when first codified at the Council of Nicaea in 325.

Other Church norms and values have changed dramatically in recent years. The Church has redefined itself, toning down its earlier emphasis on the Church as an institution in favor of a new emphasis on the Church as the "people of God." Although it has not abandoned the teaching authority of the magisterium, the Church has placed more emphasis on individual responsibility for one's own faith. While maintaining its hierarchical pattern of decision making, the Church has made more room for dialogue and shared decision making. The number of priests has declined and the number of lay leaders, including women, has increased. The Church has revised its understanding of God: instead of being seen as punitive and judgmental, God is now seen as loving and forgiving. The Church has transformed the uniform liturgy of the early twentieth century into the more culturally grounded liturgy of the late twentieth century. Finally, it has promulgated a more open attitude toward the world and other faiths.

Though some of these changes are related to the changing status of Catholics in the United States and elsewhere, most can be traced to Pope John XXIII's call for a Second Vatican Council. The Council, which took place between 1962 and 1965, reaffirmed core teachings such as Incarnation and Resurrection. At the same time, in the midst of considerable struggle between liberals and conservatives in the hierarchy (Seidler and Meyer 1988), it proposed many important changes. The changes were introduced more rapidly in some dioceses than others, and as they were implemented, the Church discovered that Council documents included many ambiguities and contradictions (Burns 1992). It also learned that some clergy and laypeople were eager to move ahead with Vatican II's vision for change; others, sometimes called "restorationists," were not (D'Antonio et al. 1996; Ebaugh 1991). Most observers agree that the Church will never return to the norms and values of preconciliar days, but they are not sure what will come of the liberal–conservative tensions that persist in the Church.

From Institution to the "People of God"

Before Vatican II, the Church defined itself as an institution. It saw itself as a hierarchical, bureaucratic organization with the pope at the top and the laity at the bottom of the organizational chart. This institutional view of Church was evident in Lesson 11 of the *Baltimore Catechism* (e.g., McGuire 1961). In the introduction to the lesson (in a section called "To Help You Understand the Lesson"), the *Catechism* said:

> Jesus Christ wants all men to be saved. For this reason, He made a *Church* (special group of people) before He went back to heaven. He said that He Himself would give this Church *power* to keep on doing what He Himself had been doing on earth. So Christ picked twelve men, known as His *apostles*. He made them the *first bishops* (leaders) of His Church. To one of them, **Saint Peter,** Christ gave the *chief* power over all. Our Holy Father, the Pope in Rome, is the **head** of the Church today, as Saint Peter was the head in his day. All our bishops are the *successors* (followers in the right line) of the apostles. The *priests* help in **teaching, sanctifying** (making holy) and **ruling** all men who belong to the Church. By being baptized we become *members* of this Church of Christ.

Observe the heavy emphasis on structure, chain of command, power and authority, and the concept of priests ruling the members. This is a very institutional perspective on what Church means. The laity does not play a prominent part in this image of the Church.

Vatican II offered a dramatically different image of Church. Instead of emphasizing the institutional or organizational view of Church, Council documents defined the Church as the "people of God" (Flannery 1992, 359). This biblical understanding of Church was followed by an eloquent discussion of the universality of the Church, the diversity among its members, and members' need to share their gifts for the sake of the whole Church. Only then did the Council discuss the Church as an organization that is to serve the "people of God" (Flannery 1992, 369).

Some clergy and laity still stress the preconciliar emphasis on the institutional approach to Church, but the "people of God" approach has prevailed in the postconciliar years. If the *Baltimore Catechism* portrayed the Church as a hierarchical institution that ruled laypeople, Vatican II documents made it clear that from then on the "people of God" are paramount and the institutional Church is to be seen as a means to help them gain their eternal salvation. Kennedy (1988) has described this change as a shift from Culture I (institution-oriented) Catholicism to Culture II (people-oriented) Catholicism.

From Compliance to Conscience

In preconciliar years, the Church placed a great deal of stress on Catholics' responsibility to comply with official Church teachings. It stressed the authoritative nature of the magisterium's formulations of Catholic faith and morals, and Church leaders used guilt to produce compliance with Church teachings. Individual Catholics were taught that they had a duty to learn the Church's teachings and, once they had a fully informed conscience, were obliged to accept the teachings. The emphasis, expressed throughout the *Baltimore Catechism,* was on individuals' compliance with an external locus of authority (the magisterium).

In postconciliar years, the Church certainly has not abandoned the importance it attaches to the teaching authority of the magisterium and the laity's need to embrace church teachings. Indeed, one of the hallmarks of Pope John Paul II's tenure as pope has been his insistence that Catholics comply with traditional church norms and values. At the same time, however, the Church has placed greater weight on the individual's need to take personal responsibility for his/her own faith. Against the wishes of some vocal opponents, it has reduced its traditional emphasis on compliance with the external authority of the Church as an institution and increased its emphasis on the internal authority of the individual's personal experience and conscience. More than ever, it recognizes that in specific social and cultural contexts, individuals acting in good conscience sometimes are inclined toward patterns of faith and moral decisions that are not consistent with official Church teachings. Even when fully informed of these teachings, individuals may believe that the right thing to do is at odds with Church teachings. The *Catechism of the Catholic Church* (1995, 490–95) now teaches that under such circumstances, the individual must follow his/her conscience. McNamara (1992) shows that this shift has dramatically changed the educational experiences of Catholic high school students in the post–Vatican II era.

From Centralization to Decentralization of Authority

In the late 1800s, there was a movement toward increased centralization of authority in the Church. The Vatican was losing control over secular affairs in Italy, and church leaders wanted to reassert their authority over matters of faith and morals (Seidler and Meyer 1988; Burns 1992). This movement led to Vatican I (1869–70) and its declaration of the infallibility of the pope. In the United States, "traditionalists" emphasizing the need for clerical control of the Church and the values of parochial schools over public schools gained the upper hand over "Americanists" who wanted the church to adapt to the democratic values of the United States. Decisions were handed down from the Vatican to American bishops, who passed them along to local priests, who in turn communicated them to parishioners. Communication tended to be a monologue: church leaders spoke; laypeople listened.

In formal terms, the authority structure of the Church has not changed since the turn of the century. The pope remains the head of the Church, and there still is a clear line of authority from pope, to bishop, to priest, to people. Moreover, many Church leaders continue to act on the basis of this pyramidal structure of decision making. However, Vatican II authorized more collegiality in the relationship between the pope and the bishops. And though Church leaders sometimes still act unilaterally, decision making is now much more democratic than it used to be. American bishops consult with their various diocesan councils and with lay leaders much more than they used to, as exemplified in the process by which they drafted the pastoral letters on peace (1983) and on economic justice (1986). Parish priests increasingly share administrative responsibilities with lay leaders and listen to parish councils. In some matters at least, communication now resembles a dialogue: Church leaders and lay people talk things over and make decisions they all believe are in the interest of the whole Church.

From Male Clergy to Female Lay Leaders

Table 1.3 shows that a U-shaped ratio of Catholic priests to laypeople characterized the twentieth-century United States. The "priest shortage" at the outset of the twentieth century declined through the 1940s (the so-called golden era), as the Catholic population stabilized and the supply of priests grew. Then the priest shortage reappeared because the supply of priests has not kept pace with the recent strong growth in the Catholic population. Relative to the number of Catholic laypeople, there are fewer priests today than in 1900 (see table 1.3). A similar decline in the number of seminarians indicates that this trend will continue well into the future. Though the number of permanent deacons increased from only 4,725 in 1980 to 12,675 in 1999, deacons cannot perform all of the sacramental functions of priests, and considerable ambiguity and conflict exist over the role that deacons should play in the church (DeRego and Davidson 1999). The relative shortage of ordained men has been matched, indeed exceeded, by the steep drop in the number of women religious (170,438 in 1960; 84,034 in 1999). On another side of the ledger is a marked increase in the number of lay ministers, especially lay ministers who are women. The trend began in the 1950s (Thorman 1962; Ebaugh 1991) and has exploded in the past several decades. Murnion and DeLambo (1999) estimate that more than 30,000 lay ministers are now working in parish and diocesan offices; the vast majority are women.

Women's role in the Church remains unsettled, and women continue to be marginalized in many of the Church's decision-making processes. Even so, women are accumulating influence. Wallace (1992) has documented the ris-

Table 1.3. Ratio of Priests to Laypeople, 1900–99

Year	Number of Priests	Millions of Catholics	Ratio of Priests to Laypeople
1900	11,987	12	1:1,001
1910	16,550	16	1:967
1920	21,019	20	1:951
1930	27,864	20	1:718
1940	35,839	22	1:614
1950	43,889	29	1:661
1960	54,682	42	1:768
1970	58,161	48	1:825
1980	58,398	50	1:856
1990	53,088	59	1:1,111
1999	46,603	62	1:1,330

Sources: Data from Gerald Shaughnessy, *Has the Immigrant Kept the Faith?* (New York: Arno Press and *The New York Times,* [1925] 1969); *Official Catholic Directory,* annual eds. (New Providence, N.J.: P. J. Kenedy.)

ing number of parishes headed by women administrators. More often than not, women are a majority of the people attending national church conferences and heading diocesan ministries.

From Punitive God to Loving God

There have always been two Christian views of God. The Old Testament image is of a God who establishes rules, and when they are violated, demonstrates displeasure through punishment. The New Testament image is of a loving God who reaches out to people, forgives their sins, and promises them a better life in heaven.

In the first half of the twentieth century, the Church promulgated a punitive image of God. It enforced strict rules that applied to nearly all areas of social, spiritual, and moral life. Catholics were to eat fish (not meat) on Fridays, go to private confession on Saturday in preparation for Holy Communion on Sunday, fast between midnight Saturday and Mass on Sunday, attend Mass every Sunday, receive Holy Communion weekly, make sacrifices during Lent, observe Holy Days of Obligation, maintain sexual purity until marriage, and use natural family planning (not artificial means) to control family size. Failure to comply with these and many other dicta was a sin, a willful violation of God's laws. Sins varied in magnitude from venial (relatively minor) to mortal (the most serious). Because there were so many laws and possible transgressions, many Catholics lived in fear of God and the possibility of going to hell.

In the latter half of the twentieth century, the Church hierarchy has emphasized a loving God, one characterized by unconditional love, compassion, and kindness. Since Vatican II, the Church has stressed God's boundless love. In the post–Vatican II years, Catholics have been taught that God expects people to love one another with the same unconditional love God has for them. According to this view, God knows people will treat one another unjustly now and then, but God also understands their human frailties. God does not punish them; God loves and forgives them. God's followers are to do the same. It has been said that homilies and religious education in the post–Vatican II years boil down to three words: "Jesus loves you."

Uniform to Culturally Grounded Liturgy

Before Vatican II, the emphasis was on the Mass as a sacrifice. Going to Mass meant recalling the fact that Christ died for our sins. The Mass was a somber ritual conducted in Latin. The priest, who faced the altar with his back to the people, was the center of attention. The laity's preparation for Mass included confession and fasting from midnight the night before. People were very quiet; they seldom, if ever, interacted. They tended to wear dark clothes, as if they were going to a funeral. When there was music, the organist and the choir were louder than the people. This pattern obtained worldwide. No matter the country or region, the Mass was the same.

Since Vatican II, and against the wishes of some Catholics, the understanding of the Mass has changed. To the traditional emphasis on the Mass as sacrifice (commemorating Christ's death) has been added an emphasis on the Mass as celebration (commemorating Christ's Resurrection and continuing presence among the "people of God"). The Mass also has changed from being priest-centered to being people-centered. As a result, the mood has changed. The priest now faces the people. Confession and fasting are no longer required. Now when people go to Mass, they tend to wear brightly colored clothes. They talk with one another. They don't just follow along; they actively participate. Although organ music has not disappeared, the contemporary sounds of guitars and folk tunes are more common. The music tends to be uplifting, and the people sing. The Mass is conducted in the language of the people and, thus, varies from locality to locality. For example, in the archdiocese of Los Angeles, the Mass on any given weekend is conducted in forty-five different languages.

Ritual to Scriptural Devotionals

In the pre–Vatican II Church, Catholic spirituality took specific forms, including novenas, retreats, private confession, Forty Hours, rosaries, Stations of the Cross, benedictions, and prayer cards. These devotional activities had a common emphasis on ritualized prayer. They called people together for the sake of sharing in a repetitive sequence designed to bring the participants into closer relationship with God. The solemnity of the activities enabled participants to gain a sense of God's power and mercy. They were to prostrate themselves and be awed by God's wondrous deeds. As symbols, these devotional practices used a combination of quiet (Forty Hours) and communal prayer (rosaries, Stations of the Cross). Incense and candles evoked a sense of wonder and mystery. The use of Latin and organ music added to the sense of transcendence.

In the wake of Vatican II, many of these older forms of spirituality have been deemphasized. To the dismay of many Catholics who love these traditional devotional practices, fewer parishes conduct Stations of the Cross, Forty Hours, and benedictions. Rosaries continue to be said by older people before weekday Masses, but are less often promoted among young Catholics. The Church has given more and more attention to a host of new devotional forms, many of which older Catholics associate with Protestant spirituality. These new forms include reading the Bible, participating in Bible study, and attending prayer groups and faith-sharing groups (such as small Christian communities).

Most of these practices express the Church's goal of increasing the laity's access to sacred Scripture. Though some of these practices (such as Bible reading) can be conducted in private, most (such as Bible study and small faith communities) are communal in nature. Rather than turning the laity's attention away from this world and toward God, as older devotional practices tended to do, newer devotional practices focus attention on the role of faith in Catholics' daily lives. There is little sense of the repetition that was so prominent a part of earlier practices; new forms of spirituality involve a great deal more emphasis on personal exploration and whatever implications flow from personal discovery. There is little of the earlier sense of mystery and wonder; the emphasis is the real world and real relationships. Instead of silence and incense, words and good deeds are the media through which spirituality unfolds.

From Church against Culture to Church in Culture

At the beginning of the twentieth century, the Church saw itself as standing over and against the prevailing culture. As expressed by Pope Leo XIII in his condemnation of Americanism, and by Pope Pius X in his condemnation of modernism, this view stressed the idea that the Church, as the fullness of truth, stood against an individualistic, materialistic, capitalistic, and largely Protestant culture. The Church saw itself as a witness to God's plan and an inspiration for others to emulate.

At Vatican II, leaders revised this Catholic view of the Church's place in the world. Instead of seeing the world and human beings' role in it as corrupting God's work, Council leaders saw the world and human achievement as signs of God's creation.

In a Council document titled *Lumen Gentium,* they wrote:

> Far from considering the conquests of man's genius and courage as opposed to God's power as if he set himself up as a rival to the Creator, Christians ought to be convinced that the achievements of the human race are a sign of God's greatness and the fulfill-ment of his mysterious design. With an increase in human power comes a broaden-ing of responsibility on the part of individuals and communities: there is no question, then, of the Christian message inhibiting men from building up the world or making them disinterested in the good of their fellows: on the contrary, it is an incentive to do these very things. (Flannery 1992, 934)

Instead of pitting the Church against the world (as had been true earlier in the century), Council leaders saw the Church as fully integrated into modern life. In *Gaudium et Spes,* they offer the following view of the Church's role in society:

> The Church, at once "a visible organization and a spiritual community," travels the same journey as all mankind and shares the same earthly lot with the world: it is to be a leaven and, as it were, the soul of human society in its renewal by Christ and transformation into the family of God. (Flannery 1992, 939–40)

Although the pre–Vatican II emphasis on the Church's countercultural role certainly has not disappeared (witness Pope John Paul II's frequent references to the "culture of death"), there clearly has been a movement toward a more integrationist view of the Church's role in society.

From Parochialism to Ecumenism

In the first half of the century, the Church tended to see itself as the "one true Church." It was Christ's presence on earth. It was the fullness of truth. Other churches were seen as "separated brethren." The emphasis was on the differ-ences between Catholicism and Protestantism. That attitude is still being expressed in many places, such as *Dominus Iesus,* saying that other faiths suf-fer from defects. Overall, however, the Catholic Church is now more ecu-menical than it used to be. At one point, the Second Vatican Council said, "the Catholic Church gladly values what other Christian churches and other eccle-siastical communities have contributed and are contributing cooperatively" to human development (Flannery 1992, 940). With this newfound respect for other faiths, Church leaders have tended to downplay the differences between Catholicism and other religions. Instead, they generally stress commonalities with other faiths. Young Catholics have been taught that they are Christians who share much with members of Protestant denominations. More and more, one hears Catholics and Protestants alike referring to the Catholic Church as "just another denomination."

QUESTIONS

The first column of table 1.1 indicates the "restorationist" tendencies that prevailed in the Church during the late nineteenth and early twentieth centuries. The second column depicts the changes that were under way during the middle of the twentieth century, mainly in relation to Vatican II. The third column indicates the "integrationist" period of the late twentieth century (D'Antonio et al. 1996). These are the central tendencies of each period, but considerable debate continues over the future of the Church in America. Some Catholics, including some high-ranking Church leaders, want to move ahead with the integrationist agenda of the post–Vatican II period. Others, also including members of the Church hierarchy, want to restore earlier patterns of faith and morals. The mixed messages from the Vatican about the Church's future direction are epitomized in Pope John Paul II's decision in late 2000 to beatify two popes with vastly different visions of the Church: Pope Pius IX (a symbol of the pre–Vatican II Church) and Pope John XXIII (a symbol of the post–Vatican II Church). The long-range outcome of this integrationist–restorationist debate is unknown.

Thus the Catholic Church in America enters the new millennium struggling with a number of issues of great moment. The pope's concern is reflected in his 1999 publication *Ecclesia in America*. The laity's concern is evident in its questions about the importance of the Church as institution; the significance of sacraments and religious practices; the locus of authority on matters of sexual and reproductive ethics; the proper perspective on social, economic, and political issues; the priest shortage; and the most effective ways to make decisions in the Church. Catholics are asking questions such as What's really at the core of the Catholic faith? Is it belief in the Incarnation and Resurrection? Is it agreeing with the Church's social teachings or opposing abortion? How important is the Church compared with other aspects of life? What does it take to be a good Catholic? Is it regular Mass attendance, marrying in the Church, or loving one's neighbor and doing good for others? Should laypeople obey official Church teachings, or make up their own minds based on their personal experiences? Is abortion intrinsically wrong, or does it depend on the circumstances? Who should have the final say on matters such as divorce and remarriage, the death penalty, and selection of parish priests? Church leaders or laypeople? Should the Church limit ordination to celibate men, or should it also ordain women and married men? To what extent should decisions in parishes and dioceses be based on democratic principles?

The coauthors of this book have examined the laity's struggles in these regards in a variety of studies. In the 1980s, John Seidler and Katherine Meyer (1989) conducted their study of conflict and change in the Church. In 1987, William D'Antonio, James Davidson, Dean Hoge, and Ruth Wallace conducted a national study that led to *The American Catholic Laity in a Changing Church* (D'Antonio et al. 1989). The results of a follow-up study in 1993 are contained in *Laity: American and Catholic* (D'Antonio et al. 1996). James Davidson directed a 1995 national study reported on in *The Search for Common Ground* (Davidson et al. 1997). As part of their research on small Christian communities, Bernard Lee and William D'Antonio (2000) conducted a 1996 national study of American Catholics that eventuated in *The Catholic Experience of Small Christian Communities*. Dean Hoge, William Dinges, Mary Johnson, and Juan Gonzales conducted a 1997 study of young adults that has led to *Young Adult Catholics* (Hoge et al. 2001).

All of these studies indicate considerable diversity in the beliefs and practices of American Catholics. They also point to factors that contribute to this pluralism. However, they are limited in two important respects: they are snapshots of American Catholics at particular points in time, and they do not provide the longitudinal data needed to discern trends. They also identify factors that are associated with different patterns of belief and practice at each point in time, but they are unable to show whether these influences persist or change over time.

Now, with a grant from the Louisville Institute and the assistance of the Gallup organization, we are able to address these longitudinal issues. We have incorporated many of the same questions that were included in our 1987 and 1993 national surveys, Davidson et al.'s 1995 survey, Lee and D'Antonio's 1996 survey, and Hoge et al.'s 1997 survey into a brand-new (1999) national survey of American Catholics. Thus unlike the other studies, which focus on one point in time, we are able to compare Catholics' beliefs and practices at six-year intervals. The ability to compare answers over time allows us to document trends in areas such as religious practice, moral authority, and decision making in the Church. That is one feature that sets this book apart from our earlier analyses.

Another feature that makes this book unique is our ability to compare the responses of different types of Catholics over time. For the first time, we can compare the beliefs and practices of Catholic men and women at three points in time: 1987, 1993, and 1999. We also can compare the views of pre–Vatican II, Vatican II, and post–Vatican II Catholics over time—something we've not been able to do until now. And we now can compare the views of highly committed and not so highly committed Catholics over the years. The ability to show how these factors relate to Catholics' beliefs and practices at six-year intervals provides a unique opportunity to examine persistence and change among the sources of Catholic unity and diversity.

CONCLUSIONS

We have described major changes in the Church and its relationship with American society during the last century. We also have identified a number of issues that have arisen from these changes. These issues concern the extent and nature of Catholic identity, the frequency of participation in sacraments and various devotional practices, the internal and external locus of authority on sexual and reproductive matters, agreement and disagreement with the Church's social teachings on issues such as welfare and the death penalty, responses to the priest shortage and its consequences, and preferred forms of decision making in the Church. We asked American Catholics in 1987, 1993, and 1999 what they thought about these issues. One of our goals is to compare their answers. Our other goal is to show how their answers are affected by gender, generation, and commitment to the Catholic Church. In the next chapter, we outline our approach to these issues and indicate the significance our analysis has for American Catholics.

Chapter Two

Our Approach to the Issues:
Theory, Methods, and Significance

People's social and cultural experiences, and the way they interpret their experiences, affect their religious attitudes and actions. Sometimes their experiences foster beliefs and practices that are consistent with official Church teachings; at other times, they lead elsewhere. In either case, our analysis enables readers to understand the influence that social and cultural factors have on spiritual and moral perspectives.

Like other people, Catholics are products of their social and cultural environments. Their views about faith and morals are shaped by what they have learned over the course of their lives. However, Catholics are not just passive products of their environments; they also interpret their experiences and make decisions of their own. Sometimes these decisions are consistent with their Church experiences; at other times, they are at odds with what they have been taught. In short, Catholics are reflections of situations they have been in, and they are human beings who make choices. Their views about faith and morals are likely to be a combination of the things they have learned and decisions they have made.

A demographic profile of American Catholics points to a number of factors that might affect Catholics' beliefs and practices at the beginning of the new millennium (see table 2.1). When we analyzed the relative effect that demographic characteristics and other influences have on Catholics' views of faith and morals, we found three variables to be more important than others included in our study: (1) gender, (2) generation, and (3) commitment to the Church.

Gender

Gender is an ascribed attribute, a trait one is born with. Like other ascribed qualities, such as race, gender sets a person's life in motion. Traditionally,

19

Table 2.1. Profile of American Catholic Laity, 1999

Characteristic	%
Race	
White	82
Other races	18
Religious upbringing	
Raised Catholic	88
Raised other/none	12
Education	
High school or less	39
Some college, trade/technical school	34
Finished college or more	27
Years of Catholic schooling	
None	39
1–6	25
7–12	31
13+	5
Marital status	
Married	50
Single, never married	26
Widowed, separated, divorced	23
Family income (current dollars)	
$100,000+	7
$75,000–99,999	11
$50,000–74,999	19
$20,000–49,999	42
Less than 20,000	21
Registered parishioner	
Yes	67
No	33

Catholic women learned that an important part of their role in life was to have children and to pass the Catholic faith on to their sons and daughters. They were encouraged to internalize their faith and embrace the moral traditions of the Church. Catholic men, on the other hand, were taught that their role in life was to work outside the home and provide for their families' well-being; religion was not as important a feature of their socialization.

However, socialization experiences have changed in the last thirty to forty years. Young women, for example, are now taught that they, too, have a right to work outside the home and provide for their families. They also have learned that they have a responsibility to make up their own minds about matters of faith and morals. Though men and women have mixed feelings about gender roles, and both have changed the way they think about faith and morals, women are still more likely than men are to take religion seriously (Davidson et al. 1997).

Generation

Generation is another ascribed attribute. It is a fixed trait having to do with the era in which one is born and raised. Today's Catholics belong to three generations (Davidson et al. 1997; Davidson 2000). Pre–Vatican II Catholics were born in the 1910s, 1920s, and 1930s. They experienced the Great Depression of the 1930s and World War II. They are what Tom Brokaw (1998) calls "the greatest generation." As the label "pre–Vatican II" suggests, they were raised in the "old Church." As a result of these social and religious influences, they are more likely than more recent generations to have traditional views on social and religious issues. Pre–Vatican II Catholics were forty-seven years of age or older in our 1987 survey; fifty-three years of age or older in the 1993 survey; and fifty-nine years or above in the 1999 survey. Twenty percent of today's American Catholics belong to the pre–Vatican II generation.

Vatican II Catholics were born between 1941 and 1960. They grew up in the relative tranquillity of the 1950s, but in the middle of their formative years (variously defined as ranging from a low of eleven years of age to a high of twenty-three years of age), they experienced the social and political turmoil of the 1960s. They knew the domestic peace and cultural conformity of the Eisenhower years early in life but then came the civil rights movement beginning in 1955, the launching of the modern-day women's movement in 1963, and the anti-Vietnam War movement of the Johnson years. If that 180-degree change weren't enough, they experienced a similar "one-eighty" in the Church. They spent their earliest years in the "old Church," but during their high school and college years, precisely when they were weaning themselves from their families, becoming independent persons, and starting to make their own decisions, they experienced the Second Vatican Council and the uproar that followed the publication of *Humanae Vitae* (the so-called birth control encyclical). Compared with pre–Vatican II Catholics, then, the Vatican II generation should be less inclined to agree with the Church's views on faith and morals. Vatican II Catholics were twenty-seven to forty-six years of age in our 1987 survey; thirty-three to fifty-two in the 1993 survey; and thirty-nine to fifty-eight in 1999 survey. The Vatican II generation makes up one-third of today's American Catholics.

Post–Vatican II Catholics were born in 1961 or later. Those who were born between 1961 and 1981 are sometimes called members of "Generation X." These young adults have grown up in an economically and politically conservative period, during which federal taxes have decreased, the size of government has shrunk, and the gap between the rich and poor has widened (Phillips 1990; Kerbo 1999). They also have witnessed important changes in the roles of men and women in society, including families and the labor force. They were raised entirely in the wake of the Council. They were taught that they are on their own "faith journeys" and that they must take personal responsibility for their faith and moral decisions. As they exercise their own consciences, they are likely to arrive at some opinions that disagree with official church teachings. Post–Vatican II Catholics were eighteen to twenty-six in our 1987 survey; eighteen to thirty-two in our 1993 survey; and eighteen to thirty-eight in our 1999 survey. Forty-six percent of American Catholics belong to this generation.

Thus, generation also affects Catholics' beliefs and practices, with pre–Vatican II Catholics being most loyal, institutional, and traditional in their approach to faith and morals, and post–Vatican II Catholics being most individualistic and inclined to hold views that are at odds with official Church teachings.

Commitment to the Church

Unlike the ascribed attributes of gender and generation, commitment to the Church is an achieved quality. Over time, people develop different levels of commitment to the Church. We use three questions to arrive at an estimate of the degree of Catholics' commitment to the Church (see table 2.2). In 1999, 44 percent of Catholics said the Church was the most important part, or one of the most important parts, of their life; 57 percent said they would never leave the Church; and 37 percent attended Mass at least once a week. All three figures reflect downward trends from 1987 when the parallel figures were 49, 64, and 44.

Not surprisingly, these three indicators of commitment tend to go hand in hand. People who say the Church is an important part of their life also tend to

Table 2.2. Commitment to the Church: 1987, 1993, 1999

	Survey Years		
Questions and Responses	*1987 (%)*	*1993 (%)*	*1999 (%)*
How important is the Catholic Church to you personally? (The most important part of your life, or among the most important parts of your life)	49	43	44
On a scale from 1 to 7, with 1 being "I would never leave the Catholic Church," and 7 being "yes, I might leave the Catholic Church," where would you place yourself on this scale? (1 or 2)	64	61	57
How often do you attend Mass? (At least once a week)	44	43	37

say they would never leave the Church and tend to go to Mass regularly. Like-wise, people who say the Church is not very important to them also can imag-ine the possibility of leaving the Church and seldom if ever attend Mass. The relationship among the three items certainly is not perfect (e.g., some who said they could never imagine leaving the Church were not frequent attenders), but there is considerable overlap.

Accordingly, we combined the three items to create an overall index of commitment. To score "high" on our commitment index, a person must meet three conditions: (1) say that the Church is among the most important parts of his/her life, (2) score 1 or 2 on our question about not leaving the Church, and (3) attend Mass weekly or more often. To score "low," a person must meet two of the following three conditions: say that the Catholic Church is not very important at all; score 5, 6, or 7 on the question about not leaving the Church; and attend Mass seldom or never. All other response patterns indicate "medium" levels of commitment. These categorizations were used in the analyses of all three surveys (1987, 1993, 1999) to enable comparisons of commitment over time.

Commitment, like gender and generation, is likely to affect Catholics' views of faith and morals. The higher one's commitment to the Church, the more rea-sons one has to embrace the Church's teachings. The lower one's commit-ment, the fewer reasons one has to agree with the hierarchy's views. The Catholic who chooses to be low in commitment feels free to hold views that are quite different from those promulgated by the Church.

Table 2.3 shows the distribution of Catholics on gender, generation, and commitment. Fifty-two percent of all Catholics are women (a pattern that has remained stable since 1987). Nearly a third of all Catholics were in the pre–Vatican II generation in 1987; in 1999, only one-fifth. Nearly half were in the Vatican II generation in 1987; in 1999; a third. The percentage of Catholics in the post–Vatican II generation has more than doubled (from 22 to 46) since 1987. Scores on our commitment index declined between 1987 and 1993, but have remained relatively stable since. Whereas 27 percent of Catholics were highly committed to the Church in 1987, 23 percent are highly committed today; the percentage scoring medium has risen from 57 to 60; and the per-centage scoring low is essentially unchanged.

As one might expect, these three variables are interrelated. Women, no doubt because of greater longevity, are a bit more likely than men to be represented in the pre–Vatican II and Vatican II generations (52 percent and 54 percent respectively), while men are more likely to be in the post–Vatican II generation (51 percent). Women are more highly committed than men. Pre–Vatican II Catholics are the most highly committed generation; post–Vatican II Catholics, the least (see table 2.4). Thus, in addition to examining the relationship between

Table 2.3.   Three Key Variables in 1987, 1993, 1999

Variable	1987 %	1993 %	1999 %
Gender			
Male	48	48	49
Female	52	52	51
Generation			
Pre–Vatican II	31	25	20
Vatican II	47	41	34
Post–Vatican II	22	33	46
Commitment to the Church			
High	27	23	23
Medium	57	59	60
Low	16	18	17

each variable and various beliefs and practices, we also will explore the direct and indirect effects each has on issues related to Catholic faith and morals.

Other Influences

Gender, generation, and commitment are the focus of our analysis, but they are not the only factors that affect Catholics' views of faith and morals. Two others also deserve special mention: race and ethnicity, and parishioner status.

Race and Ethnicity.

Eighty-two percent of the Catholics in our 1999 survey identified themselves as whites of European background; 12 percent as Latinos; 5 percent as African

Table 2.4.   Effects of Gender and Generation on Commitment to the Church

| Variable | Commitment to the Church | | |
	Low (%)	Medium (%)	High (%)
Entire Sample	17	60	23
Gender			
Men	20	61	19
Women	14	59	27
Generation			
Pre–Vatican II	9	51	40
Vatican II	16	57	27
Post–Vatican II	21	65	14

Americans, Asian, or Native American; and 1 percent did not offer a racial or ethnic identity or refused to answer the question as to race and ethnicity.[1]

Appendix A compares the religious beliefs and practices of whites, Latinos, African Americans, and Asians in considerable detail and finds some noteworthy differences among them. Latinos are younger than white European Catholics, and do not have as many years of formal education. Although they are less likely to be registered parishioners and attend Mass weekly, they have more traditional views of the Church, are more likely to view it as an important part of their lives, and are more likely to have close friends in their parishes. However, they do not appear to be as well informed about Vatican II. They are a bit less likely to agree with the Church's sexual and reproductive norms (though a majority of both Latinos and whites disagree with these teachings). They are not as likely as to favor lay participation and democratic decision making in the Church. Latinos are more likely to practice devotions to Mary or a special saint, and are more likely to go to private confession. They also are a bit more likely to say that Catholics have a duty to close the gap between the rich and poor.

Black Catholics, compared with whites, are less regular in Mass attendance; have less confidence in Church leaders; are not as likely to see themselves as strong Catholics; and are less inclined to agree with official Church teachings. Asian Catholics appear to be more traditional in their beliefs and practices, and more highly attached to the Church.

The above findings are important in their own right, but racial and ethnic differences are not as large as differences between men and women, generations of Catholics, and Catholics with different levels of commitment to the Church. Except in the areas mentioned above, white Catholics and Catholics of color are more similar than different. Moreover, the relatively small number of African Americans and Asians included in national studies such as ours limits our ability to generalize regarding the effects of race. Thus, while not denying the significance of race and ethnicity and their effects on Catholics' religious outlooks, we have chosen not to put these influences in the fore-

---

1. Our 1999 survey is consistent with other national telephone surveys indicating that Latinos are 12 to 16 percent of the American Catholic population (see Kosmin and Lachman 1993; D'Antonio et al. 1989, 1996; Davidson et al. 1997; Froehle and Gautier 2000; Lee and D'Antonio 2000). Other scholars (e.g., Hoge et al. 2001) estimate that as many as one-third of the nation's 62 million Catholics are Latinos. At least some of the difference in these estimates is due to the number of Latinos who lack telephones and cannot be reached by pollsters. Even more of it is the result of problems in counting the number of Latinos in the U.S. and defining a Catholic (as someone who identifies with the Catholic faith or as someone who is a registered parishioner).

ground of our analysis. More detailed comparisons of racial and ethnic groups are found in *Laity: American and Catholic* (D'Antonio et al. 1996); *The Search for Common Ground* (Davidson et al. 1997); D'Antonio (1999a); and *Young Adult Catholics* (Hoge et al. 2001).

Parishioner Status.

Appendix B shows some large differences between Catholics who are registered parishioners and those who are not. Not surprisingly, registered parishioners are far more committed to the Church and far more traditional in their approach to faith and morals (also see D'Antonio 1999; Davidson et al. 1997). Thus, parishioner status is a good indicator of commitment to the church. However, one of our goals is to document trends over time, and we do not have data on parishioner status in our 1987 and 1993 studies, only in our 1999 study. Hence, we do not include it in our current analysis.

Before we turn to the significance of our analysis, we assure readers that our findings are based on professionally designed questions, randomly drawn national samples, and impartial analysis. We formulated all the questions ourselves. The Gallup polling organization used its time-tested random sampling techniques to select eight hundred to nine hundred American Catholics who were a highly representative cross-section of American Catholics at each point in time. Gallup staff conducted the telephone interviews. The consistency of key demographic findings (such as the percentage of male and female Catholics) indicates the reliability of Gallup's procedures and the validity of our findings. Given the size and representativeness of our samples, readers can be sure that the percentages reported for the total sample are within four percentage points (plus or minus) of what all American Catholics think and how they act.

The coauthors, who differ in their own theological orientations, have worked diligently and collectively to make sure that the analysis is as objective and evenhanded as possible. We have tried hard to eliminate distinctly liberal or distinctly conservative theological biases. As sociologists, we base our interpretations on our theoretical framework and statistical criteria. As committed Christians, we offer interpretations that we hope are useful.

SIGNIFICANCE

Our analysis has important implications for all Catholics, especially the clergy and laypeople who are in leadership roles in the Church. These implications revolve around the two axes depicted in figure 2.1.

The vertical axis indicates degree of "community," including Catholics'

Figure 2.1. Community and Approaches to Faith and Morals

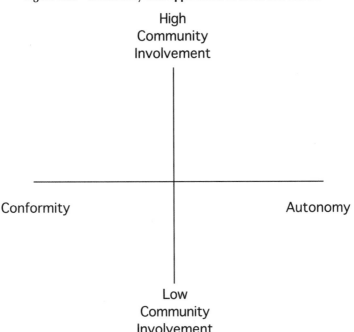

High
Community
Involvement

Conformity   Autonomy

Low
Community
Involvement

identification with the Church and the frequency of their participation in the sacramental and devotional activities offered by the Church. The top of this axis indicates high levels of Catholic identity and behavioral involvement in practices such as Mass attendance, reception of Holy Communion, and marriage in the Church. The bottom of the axis indicates very little Catholic identity and low levels of participation in the same activities. The horizontal axis depicts variations in the way Catholics approach matters of faith and morals. At the left end of this axis (conformity), the emphasis is on complying with Church norms. In this situation, final authority resides with Church leaders; individuals subordinate themselves to Church rules and regulations. Each person feels a sense of duty and obligation to the Church, without expecting to participate in decision making. At the right end of the axis (autonomy), individuals put their own experiences first and Church norms second. They believe they are entitled to participate in Church decision making and that the Church's norms and values should reflect their experiences.[2]

---

2. The community axis is rooted in Lenski's (1961) analysis of "associational" and "communal" religious involvement. The conformity–autonomy axis is grounded in Lenski's analysis of "personal autonomy" among Protestants, Catholics, and Jews.

As sociologists, our task is to indicate what the trends have been and where American Catholics currently are (figure 2.1). The trends we reviewed in chapter 1 indicate that, before Vatican II, Catholics were somewhere in the top-left quadrant of figure 2.1. They strongly identified with being Catholic, were highly involved in sacramental and devotional practices, and believed that final authority on matters of faith and morals was in the hands of Church leaders, especially the pope, bishops, and local priests. Leadership was the province of the ordained clergy, and ritual life was defined by the liturgical calendar. There was great emphasis on Catholics' need to comply with Church teachings and to "do whatever Father said." Church teachings left little room for individuals to formulate their own faith and moral orientations. Catholics went to confession regularly, attended Mass and received Holy Communion on a regular basis, married other Catholics, and were married in the Church.

During the 1960s, American Catholics took a giant step in the direction of more voluntaristic participation and greater autonomy. Along with other Americans, Catholics took part in the cultural revolution of the 1960s, with its cry for freedom of expression, tolerance of diversity, and a redefinition of gender roles. But Catholics had a double dose of change because they also experienced the shifts brought about by the Second Vatican Council. Catholics experienced not only the lifting of general cultural pressures for conformity, but also the lifting of many church rules and regulations. For many Catholics, there was a sense of liberation. They felt free to make their own decisions on religious questions.[3]

As we will show in succeeding chapters, the trends toward lower levels of participation and increased autonomy continued into the 1980s and 1990s. There are many exceptions, but Catholics generally, and young Catholics in particular, have continued their journey from higher to lower levels of behavioral involvement and from obedience to personal autonomy. When we combine the results of our 1987, 1993, and 1999 surveys, and the results of other studies of American Catholics, we see a persistent sense of being Catholic and continuing belief in core teachings such as the Trinity, Incarnation, and Resurrection. However, we also see

- Declining levels of attachment to the church as an institution
- Declining levels of religious practice
- Increasing emphasis on conscience as the locus of authority regarding sexual and reproductive issues

---

3. This shift in the culture of American Catholics helps us understand their widespread rejection of the encyclical *Humanae Vitae* in 1968. By this time, many Catholics had accepted the idea of the primacy of conscience, so the encyclical stimulated them to rethink the authority of Church teachings.

- Continuing disagreement with some of the church's social teachings
- Increasing willingness to ordain women and married men and allow former priests to return to active ministry
- Increasing interest in democratic decision making.

Conservative Catholics, such as members of Catholics United for the Faith, are concerned about these trends (Weaver and Appleby 1995). They believe that largely as a result of the changes introduced in the wake of Vatican II, the laity is either openly rebelling against the Church or gradually drifting away from it. Liberal Catholics, such as members of Call to Action, also are concerned (Weaver 1999; Dillon 1999). They believe the Vatican is out of touch with the laity and that its policies are alienating many Catholics. A growing number of committed Catholics of all theological stripes, then, seem concerned (e.g., Douglass and Hollenbach 1997; *Commonweal* 1999).

Ultimately, they all are concerned about the future viability of the Church. Conservatives who oppose many of the changes that have taken place in recent years believe that declining levels of community and conformity are placing the Church at risk. Liberals who favor new forms of community and greater autonomy worry that the hierarchy's opposition to change is what threatens the Church's future. Catholics in the middle of this debate worry that extremists at both ends of the theological spectrum might cause a schism in the Church.

We do not align ourselves with one theological camp or the other (indeed, we see the situation as far more complicated that that), and we certainly cannot forecast exactly what will happen in the long run—nobody can. However, we can show how advanced the trends are along the vertical axis of community and horizontal axis of conformity and autonomy. In chapters 3 and 4, we examine Catholic identity and religious practices to learn about trends and variations along the vertical axis of community. In chapters 5 through 8, we look at data related to the issues of conformity and autonomy. In chapter 9, we offer some predictions and implications our research has for the Church.

Chapter Three

The New Catholic Identity

The changes experienced by American Catholics have raised new anxieties about Catholic identity. We are not surprised that after the multiple transitions of the twentieth century, Catholics today are faced with new questions of identity. They now ask "What does it mean to be a Catholic?" "What is distinctive about being a Catholic, and is it important?" The main problem today is not what it was a half century ago. Before the 1960s, Catholics in the United States felt that they were being defined as different by other Americans, and therefore their identity was given to them from outside. They accepted that they were Catholics by virtue of birth, and to change that was unthinkable. The problem was how to manage this unavoidable identity. Today Catholics no longer feel so distinct, and they don't need to defend themselves against the outside. Now they feel freer, more allowed to make their own choices—whether to be a loyal church-going Catholic, an ethnic Catholic, a private Catholic, a Catholic in name only, or none at all. Now the boundary between Catholic and non-Catholic is fuzzy, and the social environment provides little "identity from outside." Today's young Catholics learn that they are Catholic, but what it means is hazy.

The change in the identity problem resulted from the change in social location. By the 1960s, Catholics were achieving higher levels of education, moving to the suburbs, marrying non-Catholics at higher and higher rates, and, on top of it all, acquiring new theological self-understandings from the Second Vatican Council. Anti-Catholic sentiment subsided in the United States. Catholics were no longer obviously distinctive. A new question arose, especially among the young and the more assimilated: Who are we? Other questions followed: Are we distinctive in any important way? Must we keep ourselves apart from other Christian groups? At the beginning of the twenty-first century, American Catholicism is in a new and different era.

31

Analyzing Identity

People talk about "Catholic identity" vaguely, often without understanding the nature of identity in general. At the outset three clarifications need to be made about identity. First, the Catholic identity of institutions is different from the Catholic identity of individual people. The Catholicity of a college, hospital, or social agency must be analyzed differently from the Catholic identity of an individual person. Our interest here is in individuals.

Second, the word *identity* is used by psychologists with two quite different meanings. One refers to the development of a strong inner core or ego of a person, as in the sentences "She has a well-developed identity" and "He knows who he is and where he's going." Erik Erikson encouraged the use of *identity* with this meaning and defined it as "a subjective sense of an invigorating sameness and continuity," or, put another way, a sense that "**this** is the real me!" (Erikson 1968, 19). The task of forging personal identity, as Erikson showed, takes time. The basics are established within the first ten or twenty years, but other parts develop in later years. Theorists in the Eriksonian tradition are more concerned about qualities of the well-formed identity, such as coherence and resilience, than about its contents (that is, whether it includes commitment to a church, an occupation, or a political ideology). For clarity, we rename this entity "ego strength."

The second meaning refers to the self as object, a personal sense of oneself that builds gradually from childhood. It is what a person sees when looking at himself or herself, or the person's answers to Who am I? and What is distinctive about me? This concept has been given other names by behavioral scientists, most commonly *self* or *self-concept*. The main point is that it is something that is observed and evaluated by the ego, a sort of portrait that the ego has of the total person. In social psychology, the discipline that has proceeded furthest into this inquiry, the terms *identity* in this sense and *self-concept* are used interchangeably (Stryker 1991). We are interested in only this second meaning of the concept "identity," and it is the sense intended by the vast majority of Catholics concerned with "Catholic identity" today. "Identity" in this sense refers to the fullest and most honest answer to the question Who am I? We will use both words: *identity* and *self-concept*.[1]

The third necessary clarification is the distinction between the identity of a group member as defined by the group leadership and the identity of the mem-

---

1. We follow Rosenberg (1979, chap. 1) in our definitions and concepts. Identity theory is more complex in ways not directly pertinent here, especially in the introduction of "salience," a situational factor less basic in personal values than centrality but more influential on concrete behavior. See Stryker and Serpe (1994).

ber as he or she feels it subjectively. The two have been called "official identity" and "subjective identity." To illustrate, consider the case of national citizenship. A person may be legally a citizen of Canada without subjectively feeling "Canadian." It could be that the person has Canadian citizenship by accident, perhaps of being born overseas to military or missionary parents, and does not embrace the citizenship. He or she will say, "Well, I guess I am a Canadian citizen, but I don't live in Canada and I don't feel a bit Canadian." Such a person has a Canadian official identity but not a Canadian subjective identity. Another example is useful but less precise: A person may be defined by his or her social environment as a Cuban–American immigrant, and indeed the person may have been born in Cuba. Yet the person may not feel this to be important to who he or she really is. The Cuban identity may be only incidental to the person's self-understanding, or even an irritant to be avoided.

A disjunction between official identity and subjective identity happens all the time for members of religious communities. Official definitions call for the people to be more, or better, than the majority end up being. The gap is easily visible to investigators. We commonly hear young people express the gap something like this: "Well, I was raised Catholic and was baptized as a child, but now I don't practice it, and I don't even feel Catholic." Or "I am officially a Catholic, but now I am not active, and I'm reading about spiritual things." Any analysis of Catholic identity needs to look at both the official aspect and the subjective aspect. The latter can be assessed only by empirical research.

Who Is Most Concerned about Catholic Identity?

It is useful to ask, "Who are the people who worry about Catholic identity today? Why?" The more vociferous are those who are committed to the Catholic faith and responsible for Catholic institutions. Their common apprehension is about the young, expressed something like this: "Will the next generation feel the importance of being Catholic as we do? Will they be active in our parishes and contribute to Catholic organizations and causes? Will they keep our churches going? Will they care if they are Catholic, or will they see all churches as the same?" These worriers want the next generation to feel their Catholicism so strongly that it will translate into fervent personal commitment to Catholic institutions. In their view, the issue of identity is really the issue of commitment. We can identify two subgroups: one is mostly concerned that the next generation have a strong grasp of the Catholic *faith;* the other that the next generation be loyal to Catholic *institutions.*

To observe a clear example of this concern, one can listen in on discussions in the American Jewish community. Concern about Jewish identity in the next generation is loud and clear. Books and articles on the loss of Jewishness and "the disappearing Jew" are commonplace. Jewish organizational leaders wonder whether they will be able to maintain their synagogues, seminaries, and community centers in the future. Others worry about the key elements of Jewish life—such as family, festivals, commitment to education, and so on. Both subgroups agree on one thing: interfaith marriage is the most ominous threat to future Jewishness. An old quip asks and answers: "What do you call the grandchildren of intermarried Jews? Christians" (Dershowitz 1997, 31).

CENTRALITY, BOUNDARIES, AND CORE VERSUS PERIPHERY

The talk about Catholic identity today is too vague to be valuable. If we want to understand Catholic identity we need to look at three of its specific aspects: (1) centrality, (2) boundaries, and (3) core versus periphery.

Centrality

To grasp the idea of centrality one must understand that an individual's identity is a structure built of elements. "Identity" is the total structure, not its parts. Examples of elements are I am a male, I am an American, I am an engineer, I am a Catholic, I am talented in mathematics, I am a divorcee, I am shy, and I am a solid member of my community. Some elements are objective social characteristics (e.g., male); others are subjective personal attributes (e.g., shy). The elements do not exist as scattered fragments but are arranged in a structure that is more or less hierarchical (Rosenberg 1979, 17–18). A small set of elements constitute a "master identity," which organizes the other elements, which can be conceptualized as existing lower in the structure. The whole thing is more or less coherent, depending on the individual. People whose total identity is relatively coherent tend to have stronger personalities, with more energy and confidence.

How is the total structure formed, and how does it change? Stated most succinctly, the location of any element in the self-concept structure is a result of how valuable it has been in serving the person's most basic needs, and specifically how valuable it has been for *achieving high personal self-esteem*. The formation of the self-concept structure is driven by a basic motivation to maximize self-esteem. This is axiomatic in identity theory (Hogg and Abrams 1988; Allen et al. 1983). All people want a positive self-esteem and greatly exert themselves, either consciously or unconsciously, to achieve it. They will experiment with this or that behavior, search for new friends, and invest more in some elements than others. As Morris Schwartz advises his young friend in *Tuesdays with Morrie,* "If the culture doesn't work, don't use it" (Albom 1997, 34). For any element to achieve centrality, it must truly serve the individual's needs. Religious leaders who want to enhance the centrality of, say, Catholic identity need to consider how this element of life truly serves the deepest needs of the person. If it fails to serve or if there are blockages, the person will withdraw emotional investment from Catholicism, and his or her Catholic identity will sink to a less important place in the structure. The process of building Catholic identity takes time, akin to making a friend or falling in love.

The individual is not fully free to form his or her self-concept because external forces always have an influence, and that influence may be decisive. For example, in a caste society or a racist society, one's caste or race is inescapable and forms a fixed portion of the self-concept. Yet in other situations, the individual has the ability to make choices and changes.

To sum up, the question of centrality in the present instance asks: Where does being Catholic fit into the total self-concept? The higher it exists in the hierarchical structure (or the more central it is) the more important it will be in determining other elements and influencing life decisions. This varies. For some people, being Catholic is pivotal and, accordingly, singularly important for the rest of their lives; for others it is only incidental, possibly a by-product or extension of some other element in the self, such as family, ethnicity, or friendships. Centrality is the ideal: all religious traditions exhort their members to make their faith central and foremost in their lives.

How can we measure centrality? Measurement is difficult and imprecise. Knowing the place of Catholicism in a person's self-concept, like knowing the place of any other element, requires observation and interaction. A researcher can always ask the person, the respondent can reply, and the reply has some value. But reality is much more complex. Even respondents cannot know exactly the place of Catholicism in their lives, because the forces structuring the self-concept are partly unconscious. The most we can do is make some approximations through inferences.

Our 1987, 1993, and 1999 Gallup surveys included three questions touching on the centrality of Catholicism to the interviewees, and all are useful preliminary measures. They asked about the centrality of the Catholic *Church,* not the Catholic faith, the spirituality, or the teachings. The responses can be seen as indicators of commitment to the Church and also as indicators of the centrality of the Church in individuals' identities. The first question asked, "How important is the Catholic Church to you personally?" Forty-four percent answered "the most important part of my life" or "among the most important parts of my life." (On this question the responses did not change from 1987 to 1999.) This tells us that for most Catholics, the Church is not "the most important part" of their lives, as they see it. It is typically not at the pinnacle of the identity hierarchy.

The second question asked if the person might ever leave the Catholic Church. In 1999, 48 percent said that they would never do so, down from 55 percent in 1987 and 51 percent in 1993.

The third question asked about frequency of Mass attendance. In 1999, 37 percent reported going to Mass weekly or more, down from 44 percent in 1987 and 42 percent in 1993. This is another indication that the centrality of the Catholic Church is waning.

We constructed a Church Commitment Index from these three items (see chapter 2). Using easily understood cutting points, we defined 23 percent of the sample as high, 60 percent as medium, and 17 percent as low in Church commitment. We found that the Church is more central to women than to men, and clearly more central to older Catholics than young ones. In further analysis (not shown here) the category for whom the Church is the most central is a combination of the two, pre–Vatican II women, 47 percent of whom scored high on the Church Commitment Index.

In the 1999 survey we asked respondents about their agreement with three statements about centrality. Table 3.1 gives the responses of all Catholics and of each generation.[2] On all three statements agreement is quite high, indicating a high degree of centrality to being Catholic. Differences between men and women's responses were small. The generational differences are smaller here than on the Index of Church Commitment in chapter 2. Why? Probably because these statements have to do with "being a Catholic," while the Index of Church Commitment measured commitment to the institutional *Church*. Young adults are more likely to identify with the Catholic faith than they are to feel commitment to the Church.

---

2. A statistical note is needed here. Throughout the book we report no significance tests on data tables, solely to make the text more readable and less complex. Nevertheless, we have carried out significance tests for all the trends and comparisons in the book, and in the text we write about "trends" or "differences" only when they are significant at the .05 level. This is the normal convention in data analysis. In some tables we include differences or trends not significant at .05, but in the text we always say that they are too small or too weak to be reliable. To illustrate the strength of relationships that are significant at .05, when comparing two of the Gallup surveys (whose sample sizes are 803, 802, and 877), minimum differences in responses significant at the .05 level are the following: for percentages in the range of 0–20 and 80–100, 4 percentage points; for percentages in the range of 20–80, 6 percentage points. When comparing small groups of, say, 250 cases in each, differences in the range of 0–20 and 80–100 need to be 7 percentage points, and differences in the range of 20–80 need to be 11 percentage points. Any smaller differences or changes may be due solely to sampling fluctuation.

Table 3.1.   Agreement with Statements about Centrality, 1999

Statements about Centrality	All	Percentage Agreeing		
		Pre–Vatican Generation	Vatican II Generation	Post–Vatican Generation
Being a Catholic is a very important part of who you are.	81	90	80	78
People who know you know that you are a Catholic.	81	88	84	76
It is important to you that younger generations of your family grow up as Catholics.	79	85	77	77

We can learn more about the centrality of Catholicism in the identities of American Catholics from other research. In 1996, William D'Antonio commissioned a nationwide survey of Catholics that asked a series of questions about "how important are . . . [the following] to you?" (See table 3.2.)

The responses should be seen as approximations derived from a phone interview situation, not as deep assessments of values. Clearly in first place was the importance of family (a ranking in agreement with all other research on Americans' commitments), followed by commitments to the society ("helping other people" and "the environment"). Prayer and spiritual matters are ranked higher

Table 3.2.   1996 Survey of Importance of Key Values to Americans

	"Very Important" %
Your family	96
Helping other people	77
The environment	69
Prayer	69
Spiritual matters	60
Your job or career	58
Your particular parish or church	53
The Catholic Church	43*
Money	31
Studying the Bible	29
Political issues	26
Having nice things	15

Source: D'Antonio (1996).
*The figure 43 is approximate because the available responses on this question were a bit different from those on other questions.

than the Catholic Church in general and the respondent's own parish in particular. "Having nice things" and "money" are ranked lower than has been
found in other values research, making us wonder if Catholics are distinctive
in ranking them low. Probably the most important findings for our analysis of
Catholic identity are the centrality of the family and the greater centrality of
Catholic prayer and spirituality than of Catholic parish life.

A survey by George Barna asking about what is really important in life provides more clues (see table 3.3). The survey agrees with others in placing religion in a semicentral location and in seeing family commitment as the most
central of all. Catholics differed from Protestants in that Catholics rated "your
time," religion, and the Bible lower. We should not put too much stock in the
details of a telephone interview on such a weighty topic as this, but the overall pattern of responses is credible and consistent with other studies.

From these research studies can we make a general statement about the centrality of the Church in Catholics' identities today? We can say that the Church
is often not at the pinnacle of the identity hierarchy. For most Catholics, it
coexists with other central commitments, including family, health, and standard of living.[3]

Boundaries

All religious groups need boundaries. Boundaries strengthen collective identity by showing clearly who are members and who are not, and maintenance
of boundaries requires clear rules and markers. Boundary maintenance is a
necessary task of group leadership (Hogg 1992).

Earlier we pointed out that official identity is different from subjective identity, and the same is true of boundaries: official boundaries are not the same as
subjective boundaries. The empirical question, then, is which boundaries do
the group members recognize and believe in, and which ones do they not? Subjective boundaries are necessary to every group and every religion, to define
the identity of members. Any group without subjective boundaries will find
that its members are troubled by questions about how they are different from
outsiders and whether existence of the group really matters. Catholicism without boundaries would have a problem of "everything goes" and an indefinite-

---

3. In the 1970s Dean Hoge reviewed research on central commitments and concluded:
"There are three central clusters, with a fourth depending on circumstances. These
'Big Three' are commitments to family, career, and standard of living. If there are
health worries in the family, health adds a fourth commitment of equal strength." For
lower-class people, career is not important (see Hoge 1976, 99). Church commitments
clearly exist in competition with other central commitments.

Table 3.3.   1991 Nationwide Survey on Important Values

"I'm going to name several things that some people may feel are important in life. For each, please tell me how important that thing is to you, personally."

	"Very Important"	
	Catholics %	Protestants %
Family	95	97
Health	84	88
Having close friends	73	65
Your free time	68	62
Your time	66	76
Religion	59	70
Your career	53	49
Living comfortably	48	47
The Bible	38	73
Money	32	31

Source: Barna (1991: 157). The telephone survey had 1,005 cases, including 250 Catholics.

ness about who is a Catholic and what being a Catholic means. This problem besets some Protestant denominations. Research on Protestantism shows that the subjective identities of specific denominations, such as Presbyterians or Methodists, are becoming weaker and weaker (Hoge et al. 1994). Young adult members of these denominations often believe that the differences among denominations are trivial.

An important point should be made here: boundaries are needed, but they have dysfunctions for a group as well as functions. They can hurt as well as help, depending on the circumstances. A main liability is that emphasis on boundaries often promotes separatism and distance from outsiders.[4] In the case of Catholicism, the more the leaders emphasize boundaries, the less ecumenical we would expect the members to be. Every religious group is faced with a balancing act of emphasizing boundaries enough to intensify group identity but not so much that interfaith tolerance and ecumenism are hampered.

---

4. The relationship between emphasizing boundaries and discouraging ecumenism is discussed in theoretical works but is not well established in empirical research. We know of no studies looking directly at the relationship. However, several empirical works have measured related concepts and have had results that imply that as specific denominational identity increases, openness to ecumenism decreases (e.g., Stark and Glock 1968; Kelly 1979; Smith 1998). It is possible that the relationship does not exist in all situations, and it is possible that Catholic identity properly understood could be supportive of ecumenism. See Kelly 1990 on this topic.

American Catholicism has seen major changes recently with respect to boundaries. Since the 1960s, the subjective sense of boundaries among Catholic laity has weakened. This occurred partly because of changes internal to the Catholic community but probably more so because of changes outside the community. The decade of the 1960s was a watershed in American Catholic history in many respects, as we point out in chapter 1. By the '60s, barriers started to weaken, and they have been weakening ever since. This can be seen in polls asking non-Catholics about Catholics; for example, asking non-Catholics if they would vote for a Catholic for president and if Catholic power threatens the United States. Polls in the 1950s found strong feelings against Catholics among non-Catholics and a corresponding feeling of defensiveness among Catholics. But after the 1960s, few such feelings were found. Anti-Catholicism has waned in public discourse in the United States. It rears its head in a few settings, such as in evangelical Protestant colleges, but not in public opinion polls.[5] As a result of the fading of anti-Catholicism, the perception of subjective boundaries is weaker among both Catholics and non-Catholics. This removed a prop that fortified earlier Catholic identity.

In this respect, parallels with the American Jewish community are strong. Jews, like Catholics, formerly had a clear identity given to them by outsiders, but in recent decades the combination of assimilation, upward mobility, and receding anti-Semitism in the United States has taken away much of that identity-from-outside. A Jewish campus leader had this to say:

> The American melting pot worked beyond our wildest fears. This is the first Jewish generation where being a Jew is an option and not a condition. If we can get Jews to feel comfortable with their Jewishness and proud of it, they will make more of their lives Jewish flavored. The Holocaust is history, not memory. Anti-Semitism is not a defining experience of every Jew. (Hockstader 2000, A19)

---

5. In February 2000, presidential candidate George W. Bush visited Bob Jones University, a conservative Protestant college known to be anti-Catholic, and his opponents charged that Bush was also anti-Catholic. A March 2000 Gallup poll looked into anti-Catholicism and failed to find a relationship between Protestant fundamentalism and anti-Catholicism. About 30 percent of Americans voiced some anti-Catholic sentiments to the interviewers, but the same percentage voiced negative sentiments about other religious groups. The strongest predictor of anti-Catholic sentiments was whether a person had any religious convictions; nonreligious people tended to be negative toward all churches, not just Catholic. The poll found little specific anti-Catholic sentiment (see Gallup 2000; Lockwood 2000). In a recent analysis, Martin (2000) concluded that anti-Catholicism is found today in entertainment and advertising but not in politics or public debate.

In the 1990s, American Jewish philanthropists started new programs to give free trips to Israel to thousands of Jewish high school and college students. The purpose was to put them in touch with their heritage and at the same time forge strong bonds among them, and thus to strengthen their Jewish identity.

Today American Catholicism has four main boundaries. If any of them become blurry, Catholic identity over and against the outside-the-border region will become confused, and many young Catholics will begin to wonder if that boundary makes sense. Two of the boundaries are within Christianity. The first is with mainline Protestantism, especially the denominations that most resemble Catholicism, that is, the Lutheran and Episcopalian. Many Christians pass back and forth across this boundary, because it appears to them as out-of-date, and because the theologies are not very different.

The second boundary is with evangelical Protestantism—including pentecostals. This boundary is distinct in the minds of most Catholics (and vice versa) and hence is not an urgent issue except among specific groups, especially charismatics and some immigrant groups. We commonly hear charismatics (Catholic as well as Protestant) say that denominations and their boundaries are only secondary annoyances; one's relationship to Jesus Christ and life in the Spirit is the most important thing. Protestant evangelicals in general deemphasize denominations and denominational rules.[6]

The third boundary is with non-Christian worldviews, most often a liberal relativism that emphasizes individual authority and downplays revealed religion. This is often called "secularism," and it includes a detachment from Christian dogma and a re-interpretation of Catholicism as only a spiritual or ethical inspiration.

The fourth boundary is in the opposite direction: with popular religion. Popular religion has existed for centuries alongside official Catholicism, but today it is most often discussed in connection with immigrants, especially those from Latin America.

We identify the four boundaries here to help define the tasks of boundary maintenance. The least clear boundary today, and the one with the least barrier to movement back and forth, is that with mainline Protestantism. It contains an additional ambiguity in that Catholics wish to strengthen the boundary while at the same de-emphasizing it in the interest of ecumenical goodwill toward Protestants.

---

6. In one respect the boundary with Protestant evangelicals is threatening to the Catholic Church, in that evangelicals have little interest in specific denominational identities or institutional church rules. Their religious identity is defined by a personal relationship with Jesus Christ and obedience to the authority of the Bible. See Christian Smith (1998: chap. 5).

As we said, official boundaries are distinct from subjective boundaries. The official boundaries have been clearly described by the magisterium in canon law and other documents. The official documents state that a person must be baptized Catholic to be a member; that adults need a program of training before they are eligible for full membership; that clergy must take a vow of obedience to bishops or religious superiors; that clergy status is not transferable from other churches; that non-Catholics may not partake of the Communion; that nonordained Catholics may not give homilies in the Mass; that bishops are part of a direct apostolic succession from the Apostles; and so on. What about subjective boundaries? Do Catholic rank and file accept the official rules and markers? This varies. Everyone knows some Catholics who are unreservedly devoted to the faith and the Church and who can clearly articulate why it holds more of God's truth than any other religion. And everyone knows other Catholics who say that Catholicism and maybe a dozen Protestant denominations are really all the same except for trivialities. They say, "There's not a dime's worth of difference, and they may as well merge."

Our surveys in 1987, 1993, and 1999 used several methods to measure subjective boundaries. One probe asked what is required to be "a good Catholic." The replies to this reveal subjective feelings about boundaries, in contrast to official definitions of a good Catholic. Table 3.4 shows the percentages of positive responses to nine questions about whether a person can be a good Catholic without believing or doing several things. The questions are listed in ascending order of "yes" percentages, so the top items are most crucial in defining boundaries. These surveys teach us something important. The items at the top of the table are seen as *most* important in defining a good Catholic, and the items at the bottom are seen as *least* important. Two items at the top are unique in that they have much lower "yes" percentages than all the others: belief that in the Mass the bread and wine become the body and blood of Jesus, and belief that Jesus rose from the dead. The Catholic laity believes that creedal doctrines are more important than adherence to what they see as specific rules and moral teachings of the Church.

The items at the bottom of the table may surprise some people. The 1999 survey respondents considered weekly church attendance the *least* important of the nine items for defining a good Catholic. Also seen as unimportant were obeying the teachings on birth control, having one's marriage approved by the Church, and obeying Church teachings on divorce and remarriage. The majority of American Catholics do not accept these four criteria as defining a good Catholic today. Most of the respondents saw the four as useful but in the end neither binding nor definitive of a good Catholic. The low rating Catholics gave these teachings may be a result of a dislike of detailed moral rules in general, not just on these specific topics. The shift from 1987 to 1999 depicts the

Table 3.4.   Laypersons' Definitions of a "Good Catholic"

"Please tell me if you think a person can be a good Catholic without performing these actions or affirming these beliefs."

	"Yes"		
	1987 %	1993 %	1999 %
Without believing that Jesus physically rose from the dead	*	*	23
Without believing that in the Mass, the bread and wine actually become the body and blood of Jesus	*	*	38
Without obeying the Church hierarchy's teaching regarding abortion	39	56	53
Without donating time or money to help the poor	44	52	56
Without donating time or money to help the parish	*	57	60
Without their marriage being approved by the Catholic Church	51	61	67
Without obeying the Church hierarchy's teaching on divorce and remarriage	57	62	64
Without obeying the Church hierarchy's teaching on birth control	66	73	71
Without going to church every Sunday	70	73	76

*Item not asked in 1987 or 1993.

trend from conformity to autonomy among American Catholics, as we argue in chapter 1. The trend is gradual, averaging about 1 percent a year, and will probably continue.

When we looked at differences among genders, specific generations, and people with high or low Church commitment in all three surveys, we found few gender differences but strong differences between Catholics highly committed to the Church and others. To depict those differences, we show the 1999 breakdown in table 3.5. In 1999, as in all the surveys, the Catholics with strongest Church commitment much less often said yes (that is, more often said no) to the questions, indicating that they see stricter requirements for being a good Catholic. Put differently: Catholics with low commitment to the institutional Church see many of its rules as optional. The item in the table with the least difference between high-commitment and low-commitment Catholics was the fourth: "Without donating time or money to help the poor" (17 percentage points). The difference probably occurs because the action is not closely associated with institutional Church rules. Since younger Catholics generally have lower Church commitment, they resembled the low-commitment column in table 3.5 more than the high column, though the generational differences were not so striking.

Our 1999 survey contained two other statements that tell us how Catholics think about boundaries (see table 3.6). The first statement, "How a person lives is more important than whether or not he or she is a Catholic," received almost

**Table 3.5.   Relation of Church Commitment to Attitudes about a "Good Catholic,"
1999**

"Please tell me if you think a person can be a good Catholic without performing these
actions or affirming these beliefs."

	"Yes" Level of Church Commitment		
	Low %	Medium %	High %
Without believing that Jesus physically rose from the dead	35	24	11
Without believing that in the Mass, the bread and wine actually become the body and blood of Jesus	63	39	16
Without obeying the church hierarchy's teaching regarding abortion	68	56	33
Without donating time or money to help the poor	67	55	50
Without donating time or money to help the parish	73	61	47
Without their marriage being approved by the Catholic Church	80	72	46
Without obeying the church hierarchy's teaching on divorce and remarriage	78	70	40
Without obeying the church hierarchy's teaching on birth control	89	75	47
Without going to church every Sunday	89	80	57

universal affirmation. The respondents believe that being a Catholic, taken
alone, means little if the faith is not lived out every day. Stated differently:
faith or devotions alone, apart from how a person lives, do not define a good
Catholic. The second statement asks about the boundaries of truth: "Catholicism contains a greater share of truth than other religions do." A slim major-

Table 3.6.   Agreement with Statements about Centrality and Boundaries, 1999

	Agreeing			
	All %	Pre-Vatican Generation %	Vatican II Generation %	Post-Vatican Generation %
How a person lives is more important than whether or not he or she is a Catholic.	84	87	87	82
Catholicism contains a greater share of truth than other religions do.	57	69	58	52

ity (57 percent) said yes. Presumably most of the other respondents think otherwise. The boundary with other religions, as defined by which contains truth, is only partly upheld.

Are the generations different in their feelings about boundaries? Yes, the young people feel less distinct boundaries than do the old people, especially relative to whether Catholicism contains more truth. Differences between men and women (not shown in a table here) were small.

The 1995 Davidson survey asked four questions useful for assessing subjective boundaries (see table 3.7). The first two statements in the table are boundary markers for specific Catholic identity, and a majority of Catholics believe in them. The third, "The Catholic Church is the one true Church," is accepted by 50 percent, even though it had not been emphasized as Catholic doctrine until the publication of *Dominus Jesus* in 2000. Thus, official doctrine today says that Catholicism contains the fullness of truth, but that other churches also contain some truth; this formulation may be less absolute than the statement in the survey that the Catholic Church is "the one true Church," but it still dismayed most leaders of other religions. The fourth statement is the obverse of the first, and the 41 percent agreeing is what we would expect.

Do men and women agree on these matters? Do the three generations agree? We found only small gender differences, but the three generations' responses were distinct, as seen in the last three columns of the table. The pre–Vatican II generation clearly has a stronger vision of Catholic boundaries than do the Vatican II and post–Vatican II generations, which agree with each other.

Table 3.7. Agreement with Statements about Boundaries, 1995

	All %	Pre-Vatican Generation %	Vatican II Generation %	Post-Vatican Generation %
I cannot imagine myself being anything other than Catholic.	60	71	54	59
There is something very special about being Catholic that you can't find in other religions.	60	72	58	54
The Catholic Church is the one true Church.	50	64	45	46
I could be just as happy in some other church; it wouldn't have to be Catholic.	41	28	46	45

Source: Davidson et al. (1997).

Core Versus Periphery

The third aspect of Catholic identity is understandable if we begin by asking a different question. If a person says he or she is Catholic, *what is it about* Catholicism that is important for that person? Catholicism includes an amazing collection of teachings, symbols, rituals, devotions, and practices that have grown up over the centuries. Some parts are inspiring and life-giving; some are inscrutable; and some are obviously so specific to past times and places that they may not apply today. All age-old religious traditions have this character. All have their mystics, ascetics, seers, martyrs, moralists, and scholars. Every living tradition needs living interpreters to convey its vital teachings to today's devotees, and the believers must somehow determine *what* in the tradition is the essential life-giving core. It is a sifting process, and it takes place both consciously and unconsciously, as a residue of lived experiences. The Catholic identity of a turn-of-the-millennium American Catholic is a result of some selection and interpretation from the variegated tradition. What is the essence? What is the saving Word? And what is purely optional? We asked the laity.

In 1999, we asked respondents, "As a Catholic, how important is each of the following to you?" We then read six elements of being a Catholic, rotating the sequence in different interviews, and asked if each was very important, somewhat important, or not important at all. (These questions were not in the ear-

Figure 3.1

"As a Catholic, how important is each of the following to you?"
(nationwide sample with three possible responses)
Percent responding "Very important to me."

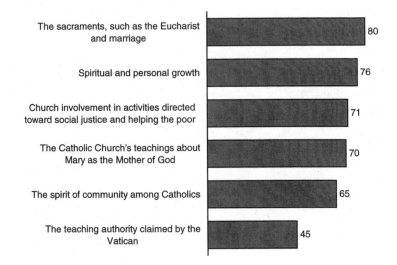

The sacraments, such as the Eucharist and marriage	80
Spiritual and personal growth	76
Church involvement in activities directed toward social justice and helping the poor	71
The Catholic Church's teachings about Mary as the Mother of God	70
The spirit of community among Catholics	65
The teaching authority claimed by the Vatican	45

lier surveys.) Figure 3.1 graphs the patterns for the total sample, and table 3.8 shows the responses of each generation.

Figure 3.1 shows that of the six elements, the sacraments were seen as most important, followed closely by spirituality and personal growth in Catholic life. Catholic emphasis on social justice and helping the poor was ranked third, and the Church's teachings about Mary as the Mother of God was ranked fourth but virtually tied for third. *Lowest* of the six was the teaching authority claimed by the Vatican, a rating of Church authority that agrees with other research showing a tendency among many laypeople to make a distinction between Catholic spirituality and Catholic institutional church life. We often hear this distinction, especially from young Catholics. One expression of it goes like this: "I'm a spiritual person, but I'm not religious," referring to the distinction between personal spirituality and acceptance of Church authority. Another common formula: "I'm a Catholic, but I don't always follow what the Church says."

Table 3.8 tells us that young Catholics rate all six elements lower than do older Catholics. On the third item, concerning activities directed toward social justice, the age differences are very small, but on the sixth, about the teaching authority of the Vatican, they are large. Young Catholics see the teaching authority of the Vatican as much less important than do older Catholics: 30 percent of the post–Vatican generation say it is important, compared with 64 percent of the pre–Vatican generation.

We looked at other breakdowns in a search for more discrete patterns of attitudes, but we uncovered little. We found that the most committed Catholics,

Table 3.8. Six Elements of Being Catholic, 1999

"As a Catholic, how important is each of the following to you? Would you say very important, somewhat important, or not important at all?"

	"Very Important"		
	Pre-Vatican Generation %	Vatican II Generation %	Post-Vatican Generation %
The sacraments, such as the Eucharist and marriage	90	84	73
Spirituality and personal growth	78	82	71
Church involvement in activities Directed toward social justice And helping the poor	77	70	69
The Catholic Church's teachings about Mary as the Mother of God	83	72	62
The spirit of community among Catholics	71	70	56
The teaching authority claimed by the Vatican	64	45	30

compared with others, had the same rank ordering of the six elements. Also men and women were in agreement.

We can learn more about core versus periphery by looking at a 1997 nation-wide poll of young Catholics twenty to thirty-nine years old (Dinges et al. 1998). Its findings were similar to the findings shown in table 3.8, except that nineteen elements of Catholicism, not just six, were rated. The interviewer said, "I have some questions about different elements of the Catholic faith. Some of these elements may be more important to you than others. How essential is each element to YOUR vision of what the Catholic faith is?" Figure 3.2 illustrates the percentage answering "essential" to each of the 19 elements, which are arranged in the order of their importance as seen by the interviewees. The highest-ranking elements were the sacraments and special attention to helping the poor, four of the top five elements. The other high-ranking one was devotion to Mary the Mother of God (fourth). The five lowest-ranked elements had to do with (1) specific moral teachings (the right of workers to unionize, the death penalty, and abortion) and (2) specific institutional rules (that only men can be priests and that priests must be celibate). The 1997 Dinges research team did not include a question about birth control teachings because official Church teachings about birth control are so widely ignored by young Catholics that the researchers expected it to be ranked very low, and including it in the survey would be a waste of resources.

To summarize figure 3.2: the elements seen as most essential to the Catholic faith are the sacraments and special attention to the poor of the world; moderately essential elements are the Church's present institutional arrangements; and least important are specific moral teachings and specific rules about the priesthood. As we found in our 1999 survey, theologically central topics were ranked as more essential than topics related to the institutional Church.

This research on core versus periphery in the Catholic faith as felt by the laity contains an important finding for Church leaders: they need to know the core of the faith as seen by the laity, since the core is the portion most strongly held. The core of the faith is unchangeable. Peripheral portions of the faith are different. They are not seen as God-given and essential. Thus they are open to debate, especially as to whether they are or are not serving to enhance the core. The laity sees peripheral elements as containing a dash of historical specificity and arbitrariness that renders them less than absolute rules today; they are not eternal truths or changeless rules for the Church. Laypeople can be expected to welcome discussing them to see if they are still serving the mission of the Church and the needs of the faithful. If not, reforms may be worth considering to help the peripheral elements better serve the core. Topics such as celibacy for priests are clearly seen as peripheral by American Catholics.

Figure 3.2

"How essential is each of these elements
to your vision of what the Catholic faith is?"
Percent responding "Essential to the faith" (Catholics 20-39, 1997)

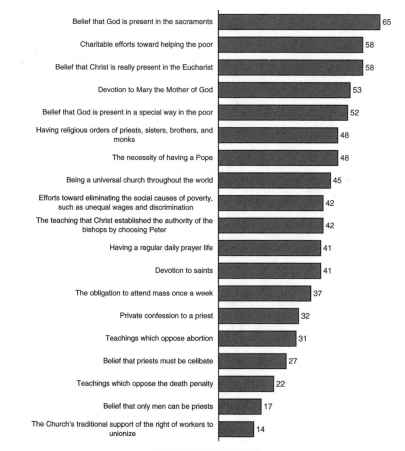

CONCLUSIONS

The distinction between official teachings and subjective beliefs is elemental. It applies to core versus periphery as well as to centrality and boundaries. The official Church teachings contain definitions of the essential core and the boundaries of the faith, but laity may see it differently. Our contribution in this research is that we provide an assessment of subjective identity. We looked at the centrality of Catholic identity in the total structure, subjective boundaries to Catholic identity, and attitudes of core versus periphery. We have seen that Catholics vary widely in how central being Catholic is to their personal identities, but the most common situation is that Catholic identity is in competition with other important commitments.

We looked at subjective boundaries and found that creedal beliefs are much more important in defining a good Catholic than weekly churchgoing or obedience to Church rules about birth control, marriage, or divorce. Catholic laypeople distinguish between what they see as God's law and Church law. The former is the valid criterion for who is a good Catholic. Young Catholics, when defining a "good Catholic," pay much less attention to adherence to Catholic teachings regarding birth control and abortion than do their elders. They appear to see the teachings about sexuality as not binding. Generally, young Catholics have a vision of Catholicism that includes less church authority and less rigid boundaries than is the case with older Catholics. Differences between men and women were small.

The research on core versus periphery agrees: Catholics distinguish faith from the rules of the institutional Church. The latter are judged to be less crucial, less authoritative, and more open to question. Also the teaching authority of the Vatican is seen as more peripheral than the sacraments, spirituality, and action for social justice. This, then, is a basic finding: in their Catholic identity, laypeople today distinguish between having Catholic *faith* and being committed to the institutional *Church*. Some Catholics are committed to both; others to faith only.

An important practical question remains: How can the centrality of Catholicism can be increased among American Catholics? We can get clues from past research on personal identity. All analysts agree that the centrality of any element is a product of how it has served the genuine needs of the person in the past. Over time, the Church and the faith become central to people who experience deep gratification and affirmation from them—spiritual, intellectual, and social. It follows that Catholic teaching, especially to the young, must have these goals and must avoid negative appeals to obligation, duty, or guilt.

Some choosing and sifting is inevitable. It is a sociological axiom that changes in society put pressure on any religious tradition, be it Catholicism, Judaism, or whatever, and this causes the faithful to ask what really is important and what must be defended and preserved at all cost. In such times, not everything from the past can be kept in place. Parts of the received faith that are not so important may become optional or may change. Nobody should see this sorting-out process as sinister or threatening. To some it may feel dangerous, but such an evaluation overlooks the new spiritual energies that can be created and mobilized in new formulations of the faith. A constant sorting out of core and periphery is beneficial in the long run, and it should be accepted as a sign of vitality in a living tradition.

Chapter Four

Religious Practices: Catholics' Participation in the Sacraments and Devotional Activities

Now that we have seen what Catholics deem the core elements of their faith, we turn our attention to how they actually practice it. There is a widespread perception that regardless of what Catholics may believe, they are not practicing their faith as much as they used to. Is there any foundation to this perception? What are the trend lines in Catholics' participation in the Eucharist, the sacrament of Reconciliation, and the sacrament of Marriage? What about Catholics' involvement in devotional practices such as praying the rosary, reading the Bible, and praying to Mary and various saints? Is participation in all of these sacramental and devotional practices changing?

A second concern in this chapter has to do with the relationship among these various practices. To what extent do they form a cohesive set of religious practices, with participation in any one type of practice being closely linked to participation in others? Or are these practices only loosely connected, with Catholics being actively involved in some but not others? Which practices are at the core of what Catholics mean when they talk about being a "practicing Catholic"?

A third concern relates to variations in religious practice. To what extent are gender, generation, and commitment to the Church linked to variations in Catholics' religious practices? Is it still true that Catholic women are more religious than Catholic men? Where are the biggest generational gaps in religious practice: between the pre–Vatican II and Vatican II generations, or between the Vatican II and post–Vatican II generations? In what way does Catholics' commitment to the Church affect their participation in the sacraments and devotional activities?

As we present data relating to each of these questions, we confirm some previous research findings and challenge others. We establish certain facts and shatter certain myths about Catholics' religious practices.

PARTICIPATION IN THE SACRAMENTS

According to the *Catechism of the Catholic Church* (#1113), "The whole liturgical life of the Church revolves around the Eucharistic sacrifice and the sacraments. There are seven sacraments in the Church: Baptism, Confirmation or
Chrismation, Eucharist, Penance, Anointing of the Sick, Holy Orders, and
Matrimony" (*Catechism* 1995, 315). In the Church's words, sacraments "are
the signs and instruments by which the Holy Spirit spreads the grace of Christ
the head throughout the Church which is his Body" (*Cathechism* 1995, 222
[#774]). They "give growth and healing to Christ's members" (*Cathechism*
1995, 230 [#798]). Sacraments "are sacred links uniting the faithful with one
another and binding them to Jesus Christ" (*Cathechism* 1995, 269 [#950]).
They are administered by priests to persons who choose to participate in them
(*Catechism* 1995, 320 [#1132, 1133])

Our analysis focuses on three sacraments: Eucharist, Marriage, and Reconciliation (Penance).[1] Given the importance the Church attaches to these three
sacraments, we look to see whether the laity shares the Church's view of them,
how often the laity participates in them, and who among the laity is most likely
to participate in them.

The Eucharist

Previous research shows that about three-quarters of American Catholics
attended Mass weekly in the 1940s and 1950s.[2] In 1961, one year before the
Second Vatican Council, 71 percent of Catholics went to Mass weekly (Gallup
and Castelli 1987, 194). In 1966, the year after the Council, the weekly Mass
attendance rate was 68 percent; in 1968, 65 percent; in 1969, 63 percent; in
1971, 57 percent; between 1973 and 1976, 54 percent to 55 percent; in 1978,

---

1. Baptism (considered the "gate by which we enter the Church" [*Catechism* 1995
#950]) usually is administered only once and then usually to infants; it is not some-
thing that adult Catholics participate in on a recurring basis. Similarly, because Confirmation is administered to each Catholic only once, and then usually to teenagers,
who are not included in our sample, we do not consider it here (see Hoge et al. 2001,
for more on Confirmation). Because Holy Orders is conferred only on celibate men
entering the priesthood, it does not apply to laypeople. And, because the Anointing of
the Sick is usually administered to persons who are physically, emotionally, and men-
tally incapacitated—most often the terminally ill, we do not examine it here.
2. The studies and weekly Mass attendance rates they report are Bultena (1949), 80
percent; Fichter (1951), 79 percent; Wright and Hyman (1958), 69 percent; Lazerwitz
(1961), 75 percent; and Lenski (1961), 77 percent.

52 percent; and through 1985, it hovered between 51 percent and 53 percent (Gallup and Castelli 1987, 194–95). The Mass attendance rate was down to 44 percent in 1987, then 43 percent in both 1993 and 1995 (D'Antonio et al. 1989, 1996; Davidson et al. 1997). Data from our 1999 survey show that weekly Mass attendance has dropped to 37 percent.

Sander's (2000) analysis of General Social Survey data further confirms this downward trend in Mass attendance. Sander reaches two other important conclusions: the decline has been steeper for Catholics than for Protestants, and it has occurred in all age categories, except for Catholics who are sixty-five or older. As a result, compared with Catholics in the 1940s and 1950s, only about half as many of today's Catholics are attending Mass weekly.[3]

Why has Mass attendance declined? Three interpretations have been offered. First, the fact that the Mass attendance rate slipped from about 75 percent in the 1940s and 1950s to 71 percent in 1961 suggests that forces such as Catholics' assimilation into the cultural individualism of the United States were beginning to erode Catholics' compliance with Church norms well before the first session of Vatican II in 1962. Second, in the wake of Vatican II, church leaders softened the pre–Vatican II emphasis on obligation and duty as motivations for attending Mass, replacing it with more emphasis on the importance of the individual's personal decision to attend. In Morris's (1997, 308) words: "Following Vatican II, skipping Sunday Mass was quietly, if unofficially, dropped from the Catholic catalog of mortal sins. . . . Rightly or wrongly, most Catholics apparently feel that once- or twice-a-month Mass attendance keeps them in sufficient touch with their religion." Finally, many Catholics were alienated by Pope Paul VI's decision in the encyclical *Humanae Vitae* to uphold the Church's traditional ban on artificial birth control over and against the advice of his own birth control commission. According to Greeley (1977, 1990), Catholics lost confidence in the Church hierarchy, a loss that was expressed in declining attendance at Mass.

As a consequence, fewer and fewer Catholics are putting themselves in a position to receive Holy Communion on a regular basis. But because attending Mass and receiving Communion are quite different actions, we also need to plot the frequency with which Catholics receive Communion. In the pre–Vatican II 1950s, regular private confession was expected, and Catholics were required to fast from food and water from the previous midnight until Communion. Under these circumstances, about 43 percent received Holy Communion

---

3. Hadaway, Marler, and Chaves (1993) and Chaves and Cavendish (1994) suggest that Mass attendance may be even lower than these surveys suggest. For a variety of reasons we have summarized elsewhere (*The Catholic Moment* 1995), we believe our survey results are more indicative of Catholics' actual practices than the lower rates reported by these colleagues.

weekly (Fichter 1951). Catholics receiving Communion often had to climb over several people occupying the same pew to get to the aisle leading to the Communion rail. Dividing the frequency of Communion (figured at 43 percent weekly) by the frequency of Mass attendance (at 75 percent weekly), we estimate that the Communion rate was only 57 percent of the Mass attendance rate.

In the post–Vatican II 1990s, private confession was not stressed as much and extended fasting was no longer required.[4] Although prerequisites had been loosened and new rules made Communion more accessible to more Catholics, only 36 percent received Holy Communion weekly in 1995. Dividing the frequency of Communion (36 percent weekly) by the frequency of Mass attendance (43 percent weekly), we conclude that the Communion rate was 84 percent of the Mass attendance rate. Catholics going to Communion were not having to climb over many people.

Does the fact that less than 40 percent of Catholics now attend Mass and receive Communion weekly signal a decline in Catholics' belief in the Real Presence? Although there certainly has been some lessening (Steinfels 1994), most recent studies indicate that Catholics continue to believe that the bread and wine actually become the body and blood of Christ.

Davidson and his colleagues' 1994 survey of Indiana Catholics asked parishioners whether they agreed or disagreed with the statement "In Mass, the bread and wine actually become the body and blood of Christ." Eighty-seven percent agreed; 7 percent were uncertain; and 6 percent disagreed. In 1997, Dean Hoge, William Dinges, Mary Johnson, and Juan Gonzales used the same item in a national survey of American Catholics; more than 80 percent of the respondents agreed. Hoge (1999, 17) reports that "all age groups," including young adults, "agreed that in the Mass the bread and wine are actually transformed into the body and blood of Christ." Also, in 1997, the Roper polling organization found that 82 percent of American Catholics believe that "the bread and wine used in Mass are actually transformed into the body and blood of Jesus Christ."

Catholics also consider the Real Presence to be among the core elements of their personal faith. In a 1995 national survey, Davidson and his colleagues asked American Catholics about the importance they attach to a variety of beliefs, including that "in Mass, the bread and wine actually become the body and blood of Christ." Sixty-three percent of Catholics said this belief is "very

---

4. The Code of Canon Law 919, #1, now states: "One who is to receive the Most Holy Eucharist is to abstain from food or drink, with the exception only of water or medicine, for at least the period of one hour before Holy Communion."

important" to them personally; another 14 percent, "fairly important"; 9 percent, "somewhat important"; and 12 percent, "not very important."

Dinges et al. (1998) did a study of 20- to 39-year-old Catholics' beliefs and practices, asking young adult Catholics what they consider "essential to the faith." Two of the three items young adults rated most highly were "belief that God is present in the sacraments," and "belief that Christ is really present in the Eucharist." Eighty percent of young adults who attend Mass regularly and 65 percent of all young Catholics said that "belief that God is present in the sacraments" is essential; 74 percent of regular attenders and 58 percent of all young adults said that "belief that Christ is really present in the Eucharist" is an essential part of their faith.

In our 1999 survey, 80 percent of Catholics said "sacraments such as Eucharist and marriage" are "very important"; 16 percent said "somewhat important"; only 4 percent said "not important at all." When we asked Catholics what it takes to be a good Catholic, 60 percent said one cannot be a good Catholic "without believing that in the Mass, the bread and wine actually become the body and blood of Jesus." As we saw in chapter 3, Catholics attach more importance to the Eucharist than they do to many other beliefs and practices, such as the Church's teachings about divorce and remarriage and its teachings about birth control.

In short, the latest research indicates that a majority of Catholics agree with the Church's teaching that the bread and wine actually become the body and blood of Christ, and they continue to attach great importance to this core Church doctrine.

Marriage

The *Catechism of the Catholic Church* clearly states the Church's view of marriage as a sacrament in the following passages:

> On the threshold of his public life Jesus performs his first sign—at his mother's request—during a wedding feast. The Church attaches great importance to Jesus' presence at the wedding at Cana. She sees in it the confirmation of the goodness of marriage and the proclamation that thenceforth marriage will be an efficacious sign of Christ's presence. (*Catechism* 1995, 449–50 [#1613])

> The entire Christian life bears the mark of the spousal love of Christ and the Church. Already Baptism, the entry into the People of God, is a nuptial mystery; it is so to speak the nuptial bath which precedes the wedding feast, the Eucharist. Christian marriage in its turn becomes an efficacious sign, the sacrament of the covenant of Christ and the Church. Since it signifies and communicates grace, marriage between baptized persons is a true sacrament of the New Covenant. (*Catechism* 1995, 451 [#1617])

Our research focuses on two issues related to the sacrament of marriage. How many Catholics choose to marry Catholics, and how many choose to marry in the Church?

Studies of Catholics' marriages consistently show that a majority of Catholics are married to Catholics (Glenn 1982; Johnson 1987; McCutcheon 1988; Kalmijn 1991; Sander 1993). Our 1999 survey confirms this finding (table 4.1): 71 percent of Catholics who are married have a Catholic spouse and, hence, are involved in *intrafaith* marriages; 29 percent of married Catholics have a non-Catholic spouse and, hence, are involved in *interfaith* marriages.[5]

There are two types of intrafaith marriages. Fifty-six percent of Catholics are in *purely intrafaith* marriages between two Catholics, each of whom was born into a Catholic family or converted to Catholicism prior to marriage. Fifteen percent are in *currently intrafaith* marriages in which a cradle Catholic married a non-Catholic who converted at the time of the marriage or later, or, in only a handful of cases, both spouses are adult converts. There also are two types of interfaith marriages. Twenty-seven percent of Catholics are in *purely interfaith* marriages involving a cradle Catholic and a non-Catholic. Two percent are in *currently interfaith* marriages, where an adult convert is married to a non-Catholic.

Our 1999 data (see table 4.2) extend our understanding of Catholic marriage practices in several new directions. For one thing, they indicate that 70 percent of Catholics are in marriages that have been approved by the Church (that is, have been recorded in a parish office and witnessed by a priest or deacon). Twenty-nine percent of Catholics are in marriages that have taken place "outside the Church" (that is, have not been recorded or witnessed by a priest or deacon). Eighty-three percent of Catholics in intrafaith marriages report that their marriages have been authorized by the Church, compared with only 41 percent of Catholics who are in interfaith marriages. People in purely intrafaith marriages (84 percent) are most likely to report that their marriages were sanctioned by the Church. They are followed by people in currently intrafaith marriages (78 percent), people in purely interfaith marriages (43 percent), and people in currently interfaith marriages (only 25 percent). People in currently interfaith marriages are most likely to have been married outside the Church.

Table 4.2 also shows that 86 percent of Catholics in intrafaith marriages are still married or have been widowed; only 14 percent are either divorced or sep-

---

5. We do not know whether the respondents' current marriages are first marriages, but, given the data we present later, we assume that is the case for the vast majority. We also include people who were married but who are no longer married, as well as people who are currently married.

Table 4.1. Type of Marriage, American Catholics, 1999

Type	Subtype	Religion of Respondent	Religion of Spouse	Percentage
Intrafaith				71
	Purely Intrafaith			
		Cradle Catholic or child convert	Cradle Catholic or child convert	56
	Currently Intrafaith			
		Cradle Catholic or child convert	Adult convert	6
		Adult convert	Cradle Catholic, child convert, or adult convert	9
Interfaith				29
	Purely Interfaith			
		Cradle Catholic or child convert	Non-Catholic	27
	Currently Interfaith			
		Adult convert	Non-Catholic	2

arated. By contrast, 76 percent of Catholics in interfaith marriages are still married or have been widowed; 25 percent are either divorced or separated. Intrafaith marriages clearly are more stable than interfaith marriages. Although a majority of people in interfaith marriages are still married, the divorce rate among intermarried Catholics (22 percent) is roughly twice what it is among Catholics who are married to Catholics (10 percent).

Table 4.2. Marriages Approved by Church and Current Marital Status, 1999

	Approved by Church		Current Marital Status			
	Yes %	No %	Married %	Widowed %	Divorced %	Separated %
All marriages	70	29	70	12	14	4
Intrafaith marriages	83	17	74	12	10	4
Purely intrafaith	84	16	75	11	9	4
Currently intrafaith	78	22	68	15	14	3
Interfaith marriages	41	57	62	14	22	3
Purely interfaith	43	55	63	13	22	2
Currently interfaith	25	75	51	19	17	13

Reconciliation (Penance)

The *Catechism of the Catholic Church* (1995, 397 [#1424]) says the following about the sacrament of Reconciliation:

> It is called the *sacrament of confession,* since the disclosure or confession of sins
> to a priest is an essential element of the sacrament. In a profound sense it is also a
> "confession"—acknowledgement and praise—of the holiness of God and of his
> mercy toward sinful man.
> It is called the *sacrament of forgiveness,* since by the priest's sacramental absolu-
> tion God grants the penitent "pardon and peace."
> It is called the *sacrament of Reconciliation,* because it imparts to the sinner the love
> of God who reconciles: "Be reconciled to God." He who lives by God's merciful love
> is ready to respond to the Lord's call: "Go first be reconciled to your brother."

Anecdotal, and often hilarious, evidence, such as *Growing Up Catholic*
(O'Meara et al. 1985), suggests that a very high percentage of Catholics went
to confession regularly in the 1940s and 1950s. In *Roman Catholicism in
America,* Chester Gillis (1999, 169) offers this vivid description of the con-
fessional experience of the pre–Vatican II era:

> In the recent past, before Vatican II, many Catholics would go to confession weekly,
> usually on Saturday afternoons in a dimly lighted church. Penitents would wait,
> kneeling in pews alongside a confessional box where a priest would sit for hours hear-
> ing confessions, forgiving sins, and meting out penances usually requiring the peni-
> tent to say a certain number of Hail Marys and Our Fathers. There would be several
> confessionals in the church, each with a name over the door identifying the priest
> inside the confessional. Upon entering the box, the penitent would begin by saying:
> "Bless me Father, for I have sinned. It has been one week or one month (or whatever
> length of time) since my last confession. These are my sins." After listening to the
> penitent's recital, the priest would briefly counsel the penitent to avoid such sins in
> the future and ask that the penitent recite the Act of Contrition. It was a prayer that
> every pre–Vatican II Catholic knows by heart:
>
> > O my God, I am heartily sorry for having offended Thee, and I detest all my
> > sins, because I dread the loss of heaven and the pains of hell, but most of all
> > because they offend Thee, my God, who are all good and deserving of all my
> > love. I firmly resolve, with the help of Thy grace, to confess my sins, to do
> > penance, and to amend my life. Amen.

Priest-sociologist Father Joseph Fichter was one of the few researchers who
collected data on private confessions in the pre–Vatican II years. His study of
a Catholic parish in New Orleans (Fichter 1951) shows that 79 percent of
Catholics went to confession at least once a year (45 percent went at least twice
a year; 12 percent went once a month or more); 21 percent never participated
in this sacrament.

As we said in chapter 1, Vatican II changed the Church's view of God. The Church toned down its concept of God as a punitive judge, instead stressing the concept of a loving God who understands human limitations and is always willing to forgive sins. The Church also changed its concept of laypeople. Instead of stressing their sinful ways, creating great guilt, and emphasizing the constant need for reconciliation, the Church suggested that laypeople are worthy human beings who tend to make sound decisions, occasionally falter, and from time to time need to be reminded of how much God loves them. The Church also changed its approach to confession. Rather than stressing particular actions (sins) and using the fear of hell and eternal damnation as motivations for confession, the Church underscored the importance of attitude and the goal of maintaining a long-term relationship with God. It also replaced its emphasis on the private nature of reconciliation with one on the communal nature of confession and forgiveness.

As a result of this reorientation, the long lines at private confession shrank. In 1977, Greeley reported that "those going to confession 'practically never' or 'not at all' have increased from 18 to 30 percent" (Greeley 1977, 127). In 1987, Gallup and Castelli (1987, 30–31) reported that no more than one-quarter of Catholics were going to confession in the previous thirty days. In 1995, Davidson and his colleagues found that only 8 percent of Catholics go to private confession once a month or more; 11 percent go "several times a year"; 24 percent go "once or twice a year"; and 57 percent go "never or almost never." They also found that even fewer Catholics participate in group penance services: only 3 percent of Catholics attend such services once a month or more; only 5 percent, "several times a year"; 16 percent, "once or twice a year"; and 76 percent, "never or almost never."

In short, Catholics are not seeking reconciliation with God through the sacrament of penance to the extent that they did a half a century ago. They are not as inclined to think of themselves as sinners in the first place, and when they do, they believe that they can talk things over with God and gain absolution for their sins at Mass or in a one-on-one relationship with their Lord.

DEVOTIONAL PRACTICES

In addition to sacramental opportunities to experience God's love and forgiveness, Catholics are invited to participate in a wide range of devotional activities, including such traditional practices as private prayer, praying the rosary, and devotions to Mary or various saints. In the past twenty to thirty years, Church leaders also have encouraged Catholics to participate in Scripture-oriented practices, such as reading the Bible, belonging to Bible study

Figure 4.1.   Weekly Devotional Activities, 1995

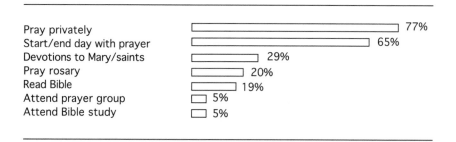

Pray privately	77%
Start/end day with prayer	65%
Devotions to Mary/saints	29%
Pray rosary	20%
Read Bible	19%
Attend prayer group	5%
Attend Bible study	5%

groups, and prayer or fellowship groups. How often do Catholics participate in these devotional activities?

Davidson's 1995 national survey shows that between two-thirds and three-quarters of Catholics report praying regularly.[6] Between one-fifth and one-third engage in practices such as devotions to Mary and other saints, praying the rosary, and reading the Bible. Only a handful are active in prayer groups and Bible study (10–12 percent are involved in these activities monthly or more).

Are Religious Practices Related?

Are people who attend Mass and receive Communion regularly also actively involved in prayer groups? Do Catholics who read the Bible regularly also pray the rosary? In other words, do these practices form a rather tightly knit package, with religiously active Catholics tending to participate in all of them, or are they a loosely knit package?

Table 4.3 shows that the religious practices we have studied are all positively correlated (that is, participation in any one tends to predict participation in any other one). There are no signs of tension or incompatibility among any of these practices. However, some practices are more highly correlated than others. The most highly correlated (with coefficients of .50 or more, marked in bold) include sacraments and traditional devotional practices. Attendance

---

6. In our 1999 survey, 71 percent of Catholics reported praying privately at least once a day; 23 percent said they pray occasionally; and 7 percent said they never pray. In a 1996 national survey, Lee and D'Antonio (2000) found that two-thirds of Catholics, and about three-quarters of Catholics in small Christian communities, pray on a regular basis.

at Mass is highly correlated with reception of Holy Communion and participation in private confession. Praying the rosary is closely linked with devotions to Mary and other saints. Praying privately is closely tied to starting and ending each day with prayer.

The practices that are most loosely correlated to the other sacramental and traditional devotional practices (those with coefficients less than .20; in italics) are Bible study, group penance, and prayer groups. The Church did not stress these practices before Vatican II but has since the Council. Apparently, these Scripture-based activities have not yet been integrated into the traditional behaviors that Catholics associate with being a "practicing Catholic."

GENDER, GENERATION, AND COMMITMENT

So far, we have shown that there is considerable variation in the frequency with which laypeople participate in the sacraments and devotional activities. Now we ask, Which Catholics are most and least likely to participate in them? Are women more religiously active than men? Are there differences among the pre–Vatican II, Vatican II, and post–Vatican II generations? What effect, if any, does commitment to the Church have on Catholics' involvement in these religious practices?

Table 4.3.   Correlations among Religious Practices, 1995

	Com	Bible	BiSt	Rosary	Day	Saints	PrGrp	PPray	PCon	GrpPen
Mass	**.83**	.34	.20	.43	.38	.43	.26	.37	**.50**	.30
Com	—	.34	*.18*	.44	.35	.38	.26	.33	**.51**	.33
Bible	—	—	.38	.33	.32	.25	.35	.30	.29	.20
BiSt	—	—	—	.14	*.15*	*.12*	.43	*.09*	*.15*	*.14*
Rosary	—	—	—	—	.35	**.56**	.26	.31	.38	.23
Day	—	—	—	—	—	.42	*.17*	**.72**	.23	*.15*
Saints	—	—	—	—	—	—	.27	.37	.34	*.17*
PrGrp	—	—	—	—	—	—	—	*.13*	.26	.28
PPray	—	—	—	—	—	—	—	—	.20	*.13*
PCon	—	—	—	—	—	—	—	—	—	.32

Bold = correlation .50 or larger; italics = correlation less than .20
Mass = Mass Attendance   Day = Start/End Day with Prayer
Com = Receive Holy Communion   Saints = Pray to Mary or Saints
Bible = Read Bible   PrGrp = In Prayer Group
BiSt = In Bible Study   PPray = Private Prayer
Rosary = Pray Rosary   PCon = Private Confession
                                       GrpPen = Group Penance

Table 4.4.   Religious Practices, by Gender and Generation, 1995

	Total %	Men %	Women %	Pre-Vatican II %	Vatican II %	Post-Vatican II %
Sacraments						
Mass	43	38	47	64	40	33
Communion	36	30	39	54	31	28
Private confession	19	18	20	28	14	19
Group penance	8	7	9	11	8	6
Devotions						
Private prayer	77	62	87	82	78	73
Start/End day	65	53	73	79	63	58
Mary/saints	29	21	34	49	28	16
Rosary	20	15	24	40	16	11
Read Bible	19	15	21	23	17	17
Bible study	5	5	4	5	4	5
Prayer groups	5	5	5	6	6	4

Note: All percentages refer to "weekly or more," except of private confession and group penance, where percentages refer to "several times a year."

Table 4.4 reports findings from Davidson's 1995 national survey. It shows noteworthy differences between Catholic men and women, with women being more religiously active in virtually every practice examined. It also indicates sizable differences between generations of Catholics, with members of the pre–Vatican II generation being the most religiously active, and members of the post–Vatican II generation being least involved in almost all of the practices.

What about gender and interfaith marriage? In our 1999 survey, gender has little effect on Catholics' marriage practices (see appendix C.4.1).[7] Table 4.5 indicates that generation has considerable effect on marriage patterns. Seventy-six percent of pre–Vatican II Catholics and 73 percent of Vatican II Catholics are involved in intrafaith marriages, compared with only 60 percent of post–Vatican II Catholics. Conversely, only 24 percent of the pre–Vatican II generation and only 27 percent of the Vatican II generation are involved in an interfaith marriage, compared with 40 percent of the post–Vatican II generation. These results

---

7. There are some subtle gender differences. Men are a bit more likely than women to be involved in intrafaith marriages (suggesting that Catholic men tend to select Catholic spouses). Women are more likely to be involved in currently intrafaith marriages and purely interfaith marriages, suggesting that they often accept marriage proposals from non-Catholic men, some of whom later convert to Catholicism. Men in interfaith marriages are more likely to have married outside the Church (65 percent) than women are (53 percent), suggesting that Catholic women are more likely than Catholic men are to insist on being married in the Church.

Table 4.5. Type of Marriage, by Generation, 1999

	Pre-Vatican II	Vatican II	Post-Vatican II
Entire sample			
Intrafaith			
Purely	57	58	50
Currently	19	15	10
Interfaith			
Purely	21	25	36
Currently	3	2	4
Each type			
Intrafaith			
In the Church	94	83	71
Outside the Church	6	17	29
Interfaith			
In the Church	48	41	40
Outside the Church	52	59	60
Each subtype			
Purely intrafaith			
In the Church	95	84	72
Outside the Church	5	15	27
Currently intrafaith			
In the Church	89	79	60
Outside the Church	11	21	40
Purely interfaith			
In the Church	52	43	41
Outside the Church	47	57	59
Currently interfaith*			
In the Church	—	—	—
Outside the Church	—	—	—

*Number of cases too small to compute stable percentages.

are consistent with most studies (e.g., Glenn 1982; Johnson 1987; McCutcheon 1988; Kalmijn 1992; Sander 1993) indicating an increase in intermarriage.[8]

---

8. Greeley (1999) suggests that this apparent trend toward interfaith marriage is not due to an increase in the frequency of purely interfaith marriages but rather to the fact that non-Catholics spouses are not converting to Catholicism as often as they used to. It is true that fewer non-Catholic spouses are converting. As the data in Table 4.5 indicate, 19 percent of pre–Vatican II Catholics, but half as many post–Vatican II Catholics, are married to adult converts. However, the data also indicate that purely interfaith marriages are on the increase, from only 21 percent among pre–Vatican II Catholics to 25 percent among Vatican II Catholics and 36 percent among post–Vatican II Catholics. Today's young adult Catholics are considerably more likely to select non-Catholic spouses than previous generations of Catholics ever did.

There also are important generational differences in Catholics' decisions to marry in the Church or outside it. Although the majority of Catholics in intrafaith marriages, regardless of generation, tend to marry in the Church, the trend is downward: 94 percent of pre–Vatican II Catholics in intrafaith marriages were married in the Church; 83 percent of Vatican II Catholics; and 71 percent of post–Vatican II Catholics. Conversely, there is a clear increase in intrafaith marriages taking place outside the Church: only 6 percent of pre–Vatican II Catholics, but 29 percent of post–Vatican II Catholics. Whereas 52 percent of pre–Vatican II Catholics in interfaith marriages were married outside the Church, 60 percent of post–Vatican II Catholics were. The trend toward marrying outside the Church also is evident in three of the four marriage subtypes where we have enough cases to generalize.[9]

Table 4.6 shows the relationship between commitment to the Church and type of marriage. The top panel treats type of marriage as the antecedent and commitment as the outcome. It shows that Catholics who are married to Catholics are more likely to be committed to the Church than Catholics who are involved in interfaith marriages. For example, 31 percent of Catholics in purely intrafaith marriages are highly committed, compared with 16 percent of Catholics in purely interfaith marriages.

The bottom panel treats commitment as the antecedent and type of marriage as the outcome. It indicates that the more highly committed Catholics are, the more likely they are to be involved in intrafaith marriages; the lower the level of commitment, the more likely a Catholic is to be in an interfaith marriage. For example, 84 percent of highly committed Catholics are married to Catholics, compared with 50 percent of low-commitment Catholics. Conversely, 50 percent of low-commitment Catholics are in interfaith marriages, compared with 16 percent of high-commitment Catholics.

There appears to be a reciprocal relationship between commitment and type of marriage. Catholics who marry Catholics tend to be committed to the Church, and Catholics who are highly committed to the Church are inclined to marry Catholics. Unlike the one-way street running between gender and generation (the antecedents) and type of marriage (the outcome), the relationship between commitment and type of marriage goes both ways.

There also appears to be a reciprocal relationship between commitment and the decision to marry in the Church. The upper panel of table 4.7 shows that

---

9. There also are sizable generational differences in marital status. Post–Vatican II Catholics are most likely to be married still (81 percent); due to more widows, pre–Vatican II Catholics are least likely to be married still (53 percent). Compared with pre–Vatican II Catholics (10 percent), Vatican II (22 percent) and post–Vatican II Catholics (19 percent) are about twice as likely to be divorced or separated.

Table 4.6. Type of Marriage, by Commitment, 1999

Commitment	Purely Intrafaith %	Currently Intrafaith %	Purely Interfaith %	Currently Interfaith %
High	31	36	16	2
Medium	56	60	56	98
Low	13	5	28	0

| Type of Marriage | Commitment | | |
	Low %	Medium %	High %
Intrafaith			
Purely	46	54	65
Currently	4	14	19
Interfaith			
Purely	50	27	16
Currently	0	5	*

* Number of cases too small to compute a stable percentage.

marrying in the Church fosters commitment to the Church; 36 percent of Catholics married to Catholics and married in the Church are high in commitment, compared with 14 percent of Catholics married to Catholics and married outside the Church. Among Catholics involved in interfaith marriages, 24 percent who married in the Church also are high in commitment, compared with 8 percent of those who married outside the Church.

The lower panel shows that 93 percent of highly committed Catholics in intrafaith marriages were married in the Church, compared with 68 percent of low-commitment Catholics. Although 68 percent of highly committed Catholics in interfaith marriages were married in the Church, only 22 percent of less committed Catholics were. Appendix C.4.2 shows that these same patterns occur when all four subtypes of marriage are considered.[10]

---

10. Commitment also is linked to marital stability. Although 92 percent of highly committed Catholics are still married or are widows or widowers, that is true for only 75 percent of uncommitted Catholics. Only 7 percent of highly committed Catholics are divorced or separated, but 25 percent of uncommitted Catholics are in broken marriages. Once again, the directionality of these relationships is not always clear. We believe that commitment has more impact on stability than stability does on commitment, but it is reasonable to assume that there is a reciprocal relationship between the two.

Table 4.7.   Marriage in/outside the Church, by Commitment, 1999

Commitment	Intrafaith Marriages in the Church	Intrafaith Marriages outside Church	Interfaith Marriages in the Church	Interfaith Marriages outside Church
	%	%	%	%
High	36	14	24	8
Medium	55	65	63	57
Low	9	21	13	35

	Commitment		
	Low	Medium	High
Type of Marriage	%	%	%
Intrafaith			
In the Church	68	80	93
Outside Church	32	20	7
Interfaith			
In the Church	22	45	68
Outside the Church	78	55	32

CONCLUSIONS

In this chapter, we have reviewed data relating to Catholics' involvement in a variety of sacramental and devotional practices. Rather than complying with Church norms the way Catholics did in the middle of the twentieth century, today's Catholics are making up their own minds about how often they will participate in these practices. Mass attendance is declining. Reception of Holy Communion also is declining (though a higher percentage of Mass-attending Catholics receive Communion today than forty to fifty years ago). Private confessions with a priest are far less frequent than they used to be, and relatively few Catholics participate in group penance. A majority of Catholics marry other Catholics and marry in the Church. However, there are clear trends toward intermarriage and marriage outside the Church. Traditional devotional practices such as private prayer and prayers to Mary and specific saints have declined but are still more common than Scripture-oriented practices such as reading the Bible and group-oriented activities such as Bible study programs. The net effect is that participation in the Catholic community is declining.

We also have shown that gender, generation, and commitment are closely linked to Catholics' religious practices. Women and pre–Vatican II Catholics are more active in both sacramental and devotional practices than men and post–Vatican II Catholics. The findings relating to gender and commitment suggest that these two factors are important influences on the ways in which

Catholics participate in the Catholic community. The findings relating to generation are important for two reasons. First, generation is an important source of pluralism in the Church at any given time. Second, the generational data point to a clear trend away from the high levels of participation found among pre–Vatican II Catholics and toward lower levels of involvement among post–Vatican II Catholics. We also have documented a reciprocal relationship between commitment and marriage patterns. Marrying other Catholics and marrying in the Church contribute to commitment, and commitment increases the likelihood that Catholics will marry other Catholics in the Church. We explore the implications of these findings in our concluding chapter.

We now turn our attention to the laity's views on moral issues and who laypeople believe has the final say on such matters as abortion and divorce and remarriage.

Chapter Five

Moral Authority and Sexuality

In this chapter, we examine the attitudes of the Catholic laity in the United States toward church teachings on sexual morality and the implications of these attitudes for the locus of moral authority in the Church. Specifically, we focus on five teachings: (1) remarriage without annulment, (2) birth control, (3) abortion, (4) homosexuality, and (5) nonmarital sex. Pope John Paul II has addressed these issues in his trips around the world. In addition to speaking out strongly on issues concerning every aspect of the human condition and apologizing for a range of shortcomings and mistakes committed by Catholic Christians, he has condemned abortion, birth control, divorce and remarriage, homosexuality, and nonmarital sexual activity. Our data allow us to track attitude trends related to the five teachings from 1987 to 1999. We will also use research from other relevant studies.

Have these trends occurred on all issues of sexual morality or just on some? Are they confined to Catholics who are least committed to the Church, or are they found among highly committed Catholics as well? What percentage of young Catholics disagree with the hierarchy's sexual norms, and what percentage continue to accept them? Do men and women differ on these issues, or do they have similar views?

THE SHIFT IN THE LOCUS OF MORAL AUTHORITY IN THE AMERICAN CATHOLIC CHURCH

The teaching authority of the Catholic Church, that is, its magisterium, has long been associated with the leaders of the Church, often referred to as the hierarchy. Pope John Paul II has devoted much of his papacy to restoring the authority claims of the magisterium. The *Official Catholic Directory* (1998, A23) describes the composition, configuration, and duties of this group:

> The Hierarchy, as the supreme governing body of the Catholic Church, consists of the Roman Pontiff, the successor of Peter, and the Bishops joined together with him and never without him (canons 330, 331, 336) in one apostolic college to provide for the common good of the Church. The Roman Pontiff in the exercise of his office is assisted by the College of Cardinals, and further by the departments also called "dicasteries" of the Roman Curia. The bishops, of whom some bear the titles of Patriarch and Archbishop, are united with the Roman Pontiff in the governance of the whole Church; the bishops, when assigned to particular Sees, are individually responsible for the teaching, sanctification, and governance of their particular Church. Apostolic Vicars and Prefects together with certain Abbots and other Prelates are also joined in this work.

For centuries, the hierarchy attended to its responsibility by adhering to a monarchical style of leadership and governance. It developed moral positions deductively and disseminated them downward. The hierarchy in Rome and in local dioceses worked through the structures of parishes, schools, and other institutions to promulgate church policies and doctrines to the laity. Letters from Rome or from the local bishop were regularly read at Mass; students at all levels of schooling were taught the Church's position on moral issues.

But the Catholic Church was beset during the nineteenth and early twentieth centuries by events that reflected modern life with its changing ideologies. The worldwide spread of democratic civil governance was accompanied by the gradual extension of suffrage to women, blacks, and other oppressed peoples. As a result, more people than ever, including Catholics, became accustomed to being part of decision-making structures. The dramatic growth in formal education, especially in the United States after World War II, enabled people to become more informed about issues affecting their lives, further undercutting systems of monocratic governance. Administrative requirements for running bureaucracies, such as the need for input from accountants and financial advisers, made it difficult for a church elite to govern without consultation with outsiders. Premises of traditional church teachings were challenged by demographic trends, such as decreased fertility and increasing longevity. The fact that women, in particular, could expect to spend a significant portion of their lives without parenting responsibilities raised questions about the association between sex and family life. While Catholics continued to maintain strong ties to family and church, they were also becoming more and more a part of American society with its emphasis on personal autonomy.

These experiences underscored the importance of certain values and their potential conflict with others. Catholics' success within a structure of religious pluralism supported principles of religious tolerance (Murray 1960), which challenged the defensive mentality that had dominated the hierarchy since Vatican Council I (1869–70). Norms of self-fulfillment and individuals' rights burgeoned. As Greeley (1973) noted, the emphasis on personal autonomy was one of the century's most important cultural developments. Professionalism and expertise gained in importance. For example, Catholic clergy and men and women religious strove to regain professional autonomy which had ranked them for centuries with doctors and lawyers as part of the professional elite but which had become diluted over time (Wilensky 1964). A steadily growing population of Catholics was also becoming mainstream American. When John XXIII succeeded Pius XII in 1959, Americans were ready to heed his call to open the windows of the Church and let in some fresh air.

Pope John XXIII wanted Vatican Council II to revitalize and update the Church to bring it into the modern world. From 1962 to 1965 it did so, as the body of more than two thousand bishops found middle ways between the most progressive and the most traditional forces. The Council, in its documents, reaffirmed the joint authority of bishops with the pope; it opened a biblical perspective toward the Church; it made important changes in the liturgy, especially the use of the vernacular in the Mass; it encouraged ecumenical activity; it fostered episcopal leadership; for the first time it emphasized the importance of conjugal love in marriage; it heralded freedom of religion and conscience; it encouraged active engagement with the larger social world; and it gave new emphasis to the laity as "the people of God, the body of Christ, and a community of faith."

In retrospect, the tumult in the wake of Vatican II should not have been surprising. Most important, the social structures needed to implement the changes made possible by the documents of Vatican II were lacking. The documents themselves did not provide more than a general idea about how to bring about structural changes. On matters of moral authority, laypeople were encouraged to believe that they had freedom of conscience. For them this has come to mean combining reason, faith, and experience to reach decisions on a wide range of moral issues (Dillon 1999). For some in the magisterium, it has always come down finally to the laity's being expected to accept the magisterium's teaching authority. The outcome of this clash was predicted more than thirty years ago: "In the long run the laity will do what seems rational and practical, and whenever the Church is defending a tradition that cannot be sustained by reason, it will probably be ignored." (D'Antonio 1966, 12).

The Kennedy presidency and the papacy of John XXIII with his call to discern the "signs of the times" were further indications of a maturing Catholic population that felt comfortable in both spheres (Gleason 1994). Then came the Vatican II documents recognizing the values in Western political democracy and formally recognizing the right to freedom of religion and freedom of conscience.[1] The effect was to encourage Catholics to think through issues for themselves rather than simply to accept traditional claims to authority. For example, for many Catholics, the magisterium's decision to abandon the rule against eating meat on Friday, while welcome, raised questions. How could it be a mortal sin for all those years, and suddenly it was no longer a sin? One older Catholic who had faithfully obeyed that rule for more than sixty years remarked in exasperation: "Do they really know what is a sin? Who knows what's a sin?"

The bishops intended to encourage the laity to be more self-consciously responsible for its behavior, but this intention was lost on many. In part inadvertently, Vatican II set the stage for the decline of the magisterium's traditional claim to authority. Rather than restore it, the birth-control encyclical *Humanae Vitae,* published by Pope Paul VI in July 1968, further undercut it.

Thus it was that within a decade after the conclusion of Vatican II, the magisterium's teaching authority and hence its moral voice was being questioned by increasing numbers of Catholics. Fichter (1977, 163–64) observed that the Roman Catholic Church was being transformed by the laity at the grass-roots level. The result has been that "dependence on legislation from above has largely switched to dependence on the conscience of the people."

We will always be left to wonder what might have been, had the encyclical *Humanae Vitae* accepted the recommendation for change made by the great majority of the Papal Birth Control Commission rather than the reaffirmation of the traditional teaching by the minority (four theologians and one cardinal) that it did.[2] The debate over birth control and especially the birth-control pill had become very public in the United States during the period 1960–68, and American Catholics had come to hope for, even expect, a change in church teachings. No event of the twentieth century so challenged the teaching authority of the Vatican as the debate about birth control and the publication of the encyclical.

---

1. Church documents have always included statements about the teaching responsibility of the magisterium and the local bishops in helping Catholics to form a mature conscience.

2. See especially Robert McClory, *Turning Point* (1995), a documentary narrative of the history of the Papal Birth Control Commission, based on the experience of Patty Crowley and other members, as well as the report itself. The actual vote in support of the report of the Birth Control Commission has been variously stated as 51 or 53; 4 theologians voted against it, and one cardinal openly opposed it. See also Thomas C. Fox, *Sexuality and Catholicism* (1995, chap. 3); Garry Wills, *Papal Sin* (2000, chaps. 5 and 6) and *The Birth Control Debate* (1967); and Andrew M. Greeley, *The American Catholic* (1977) and *Crisis in the Church* (1979).

For the great majority of Catholics, Vatican II was a positive sea change for the Church, bringing it closer to the modern world with its emphasis on rational authority and personal responsibility. In contrast, *Humanae Vitae* was seen as contradictory of the more open and self-responsible Catholicism. It was rejected by a majority of the laity and by a large number of priests and theologians.[3] The U.S. bishops stood firmly with Rome; bishops in other countries took a variety of stands, some firmly with Rome, others citing the need to inform and follow one's conscience.

The Struggle over Moral Authority

It is not that Catholics have rejected the idea of a moral authority to guide them in their daily life. As chapters 3 and 4 make clear, they continue to have a strong sense of identity as Catholics and to see the sacraments as very important in their lives. Rather, Vatican II combined with the ethos of American society to bring about a new, progressive formulation of moral authority among Catholics regarding sexual matters in contrast to the earlier orthodox teaching.[4] These formulations constitute the endpoints of a continuum of beliefs, attitudes, and values that have variously been described as integrationist versus restorationist, progressive versus orthodox, or by Eugene Kennedy (1998) as Culture I versus Culture II.

Hunter and Sargeant (1998, 45) describe the two formulations. The progressivists believe that "moral and spiritual truth is not a static and unchanging collection of scriptural facts and theological propositions, but a growing and incremental reality. . . . The legacy of faith for progressivists becomes valuable not as the literal account of historic personalities and events in relation to God, but primarily (and perhaps only) as a narrative pointing to ethical principles that can be applied to contemporary human experiences." The doc-

---

3. Greeley, McCready, and McCourt (1976), carried out an empirical study to show the negative impact of *Humanae Vitae* compared with the positive impact of Vatican Council II. They concluded that the crisis created by *Humanae Vitae* would have been even more severe without the positive gains from Vatican II.

4. In another context Hunter and Sargeant (1998, 29–57) analyze the religious roots of the culture wars that they perceive to be embroiling American society. In their work they contrast what they identify as the progressivist and orthodox sources of moral authority. Their analysis helps explain what has happened within the Catholic Church, so we have adapted the argument here. Dillon (1999, 196–97), while acknowledging Hunter's paradigm, questions whether it has led to the kinds of "culture wars" that Hunter insisted have been the result of this kind of pluralism. Other research supporting her position includes DiMaggio et al. (1996) and Greeley (1997).

uments of Vatican II, the relatively open manner of debate among the bishops that had led to them, and their reception by the public reflect that growing and incremental reality that was at the same time deeply anchored in the Catholic tradition (Dillon 1999).

Orthodoxy, on the other hand, sees moral authority as a dynamic reality that is independent of human experience and transcendent. In the case of Roman Catholics, this transcendence is communicated to the community through the pope in concert with the bishops and the curia. Jointly they "build on a shared commitment to these transcendent truths and to the moral traditions that uphold these truths" (Hunter and Sargeant 1998, 43–47). Certainly the documents of Vatican II are built on this tradition as much as they reflect a progressivist orientation.

Kennedy (1988) offers a slightly different perspective on the present-day situation. He calls traditional Catholics a "Culture I" type: "Culture I Catholics emphasize the stability of the institutional Church. They are concerned about the credibility of the Church and its persistence as a social institution." They are "rooted in the traditional, hierarchical exercise of authority." It is a characterization exemplified by the Reverend John Ford, a moral theologian and a member of Pope Paul VI's Birth Control Commission. He defended the Church's teaching on the evil of contraception in these words:

> The Church cannot change her answer because this answer is true. . . . It is true because the Catholic Church, instituted by Christ to show men a secure way to eternal life, could not have so wrongly erred during all those centuries of history. . . . The church could not have erred . . . even through one century, by imposing under serious obligation very grave burdens in the name of Jesus Christ, if Jesus Christ did not actually impose those burdens. . . . If the Church could err in such a way . . . the faithful could not put their trust in the magisterium's presentation of moral teaching especially in sexual matters. (1995, 110–11)

Culture II Catholics, according to Kennedy's typology, reflect the modern world with its emphasis on personal autonomy. They believe the locus of authority is within the believer—that God speaks through the experiences and reflections of individual Christians. From this perspective, Catholics must take personal responsibility for their faith and for living that faith in the world. This understanding of the Catholic in the modern world was contained in advice given by married Catholics in the Christian Family Movement to the Papal Birth Control Commission: "God has created us to develop our talents to govern the universe and ourselves. Since medical research has learned a method of intelligently controlling ovulation, it would seem reasonable for men to use this knowledge for the good of their own family. Other functions are intelligently controlled with no question as to the morality of the use of a drug"

(McClory 1995, 94). This perspective gradually became an accepted part of their rationale for change. In the closing session of the Birth Control Commission, Cardinal Lawrence Shehan of Baltimore expressed his support of that position: "The Church develops, and the *sensus fidelium* [sense of the faithful] plays a big role in that development. The Church must recognize how marriage is lived today" (p. 124). These opposing formulations, brought out so clearly in the Commission, continue strong today in the attitudes of the laity and the teachings of the magisterium.[5]

American Catholic Opinion

The struggle within the Catholic Church over the locus of moral authority has become more polarized as the hierarchy under the leadership of Pope John Paul II has given more and more emphasis to the inerrancy of the magisterium while the laity has moved steadily toward taking personal responsibility for moral decisions on sexual issues. Part of our research was designed to explore the laity's perception of the Vatican's teaching authority and its claims on the laity's behavior. Because so much attention in the press and in recent Vatican documents centers on sexual–moral issues, we decided to focus on the five issues that seemed most central to the Vatican's recent teachings on sexual matters. The following question was asked in 1987, 1993, and 1999:

> I would like your opinion on several issues that involve moral authority in the Catholic Church. In each case I would like to know who you think should have the final say about what is right or wrong. Is it the **church leaders** such as the pope and the bishops, or **individuals** taking church teachings into account and deciding for themselves, or **both individuals and leaders** working together?

Table 5.1 displays the findings, divided into three parts according to the interviewees' views about the locus of moral authority. For example, in 1999, on the issue of "divorced Catholics remarrying without getting an annulment," 19 percent said church leaders should have the final say, 45 percent said individuals, and 32 percent said both working together. Overall, in 1999, support for church leaders ranged from a low of 10 percent (contraception) to a high of 23 percent (nonmarital sexual relations).

---

5. Avery Dulles, S. J. (1998) argues that the cultural secularization that has created the progressive Culture II Catholicism has put Catholic orthodoxy under enormous pressure. He accepts that "in a secularized society such as ours, consistently orthodox Catholics will constitute a minority within their religious community" (p. 14). Still, he concludes that "orthodoxy rather than accommodationism [to progressive ideas and behavior] offers greater promise for the future" of the church (p. 16).

Table 5.1. Locus of Moral Authority on Five Issues, 1987, 1993, and 1999

	1987	1993	1999
	Locus: Church Leaders		
	%	%	%
A divorced Catholic remarrying without getting an annulment	23	23	19
A Catholic practicing contraceptive birth control	12	14	10
A Catholic advocating free choice regarding abortion	29	21	20
A Catholic who engages in homosexual behavior	32	26	20
Nonmarital sexual relations	34	23	23
	Locus: the Individual		
A divorced Catholic remarrying without getting an annulment	31	38	45
A Catholic practicing contraceptive birth control	62	57	62
A Catholic advocating free choice regarding abortion	45	44	47
A Catholic who engages in homosexual behavior	39	39	49
Nonmarital sexual relations	42	44	47
	Locus: Church Leaders and the Individuals Together		
A divorced Catholic remarrying without getting an annulment	43	37	32
A Catholic practicing contraceptive birth control	23	26	23
A Catholic advocating free choice regarding abortion	22	33	29
A Catholic who engages in homosexual behavior	19	30	25
Nonmarital sexual relations	21	30	26

The low support in 1999 and the drop in support between 1987 and 1999 are clear. The trend away from church leaders and toward the individual was most evident on divorce and remarriage, active homosexuality, and nonmarital sexual behavior. By 1999, on only one issue (nonmarital sex) did as many as one in four Catholics think the locus of authority should rest with church leaders alone. Between 45 percent and 62 percent of Catholics that year looked to the individual Catholic to make moral choices on all issues.

On issues where laity support for church leaders did not move to the individuals, it moved to both church leaders and laity working together to arrive at moral decisions. This was the case in 1993 especially on abortion, homosexuality, and nonmarital sex; then in 1999 the locus shifted to the individual.

By 1999 there was more support for either the individual or the combined locus than for church leaders alone.

Now that we have seen the trends, we examine the effect that gender, generation, and level of commitment have on these beliefs.

Gender and Moral Authority

Figure 5.1 displays the attitudes of Catholic men and women. The first notable finding is the rather low level of support for church leaders among both sexes, with support among women even lower than that among men. Among men, the level of support remained below 35 percent on the five issues; among women, it remained below 25 percent. During this time support shifted away from "laity and church leaders working together" to individuals alone. (The data are not shown here.) By 1999, the percentages of women who would look to their own consciences ranged from 43 percent (divorce and remarriage) to 64 percent (contraceptive use). In 1999 the men were similar, with a range between 45 percent (divorce and remarriage) and 61 percent (contraceptive use). In sum, on issues regarding marriage and sexuality, Catholic men and women over time placed the proper locus of moral authority more and more with the individual, but with variations from issue to issue.

Moral Authority Across Generations

Table C.5.1 (appendix C) summarizes the attitudes of the three generations.[6] Figure 5.2 shows the percent of each generation saying that moral authority resides with church leaders. There is a general, but not perfectly linear, decline in support of church leaders alone as the source of moral authority regardless of the item being asked about. For example, while one in three older Catholics in 1987 looked to church leaders as the locus of authority on the matter of remarriage after divorce, by 1999 the proportion had fallen to one in four. In 1987, between 42 percent and 47 percent of the older Catholics identified church leaders as the sole source of moral authority on abortion, homosexuality, and nonmarital sex. By 1999, the percentages had all fallen below 40 percent. Similar patterns are found among the other two generations, with post–Vatican II Catholics being the least likely to look to church leaders as the source of moral authority—fewer than 15 percent on all questions in 1999. Church leaders lost support among all three generations across time, but trends among the generations themselves varied. The

---

6. Appendix C provides additional tables that may be of interest to some readers; here in the text we discuss only the main trends.

Figure 5.1.   Catholic Men and Women Who Look to Church Leaders as the Locus of Moral Authority, 1987 and 1999 (in percent)

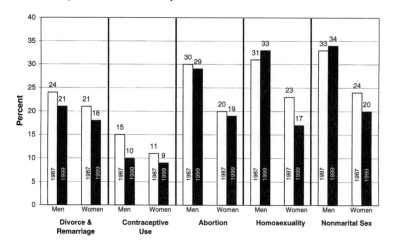

oldest Catholics moved closer to Vatican II Catholics in the later surveys. But, if anything, the gap widened between those two generations and the youngest Catholics. By 1999, no more than one in seven of the Gen X Catholics would look to church leaders as the locus of moral authority on these issues.

The trend away from reliance on church leaders is clear when we look at the patterns supporting "individuals alone" as the proper source of moral authority

Figure 5.2.   Catholics Who Look to Church Leaders as the Locus of Moral Authority, by Generation, 1987 and 1999 (in percent)

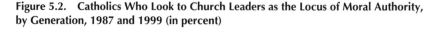
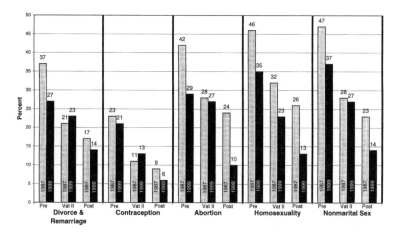

(figure 5.3). Two findings stand out. First, there were dramatic changes between 1987 and 1999 regarding divorce and remarriage and homosexuality, whereby all three generations placed increasing responsibility with the individual. Second, the pattern of change toward individual conscience was most pronounced for the oldest (Pre–Vatican II) generation. Among these Catholics, the percentages supporting the use of individual conscience increased on all five issues. The two largest increases involved divorce and remarriage without an annulment (an increase of 16 percentage points) and the morality of active homosexuality (an increase of 18 points).

Figure 5.4 summarizes the changes from 1987 to 1999 in two generations on the question of free choice regarding abortion. The top half shows how the pre–Vatican II generation changed during those twelve years, and the bottom half depicts the post–Vatican II generation. Both generations shifted somewhat from seeing the final locus of moral authority with church leaders to seeing it with both church leaders and individuals working together. Also the percentage saying "individuals" rose. These pie charts depict each generational group at two points in time, thus we can see how each changed. The Vatican II generation is not shown, but it is similar.

In sum, authority has shifted away from church leaders and toward the individual in all three generations. Contrary to common wisdom suggesting that older Catholics are unwilling or unable to change their views, we found that many have changed. Also, trends by generation were matters of degree. For all three generations, the shift in the locus of authority to the individual was clearest on homosexuality and divorce and remarriage. By 1999, support for

Figure 5.3. Catholics Who Look to Themselves as the Locus of Moral Authority, by Generation, 1987 and 1999 (in percent)

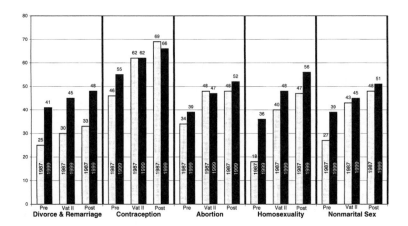

Figure 5.4.   Locus of Moral Authority on Abortion

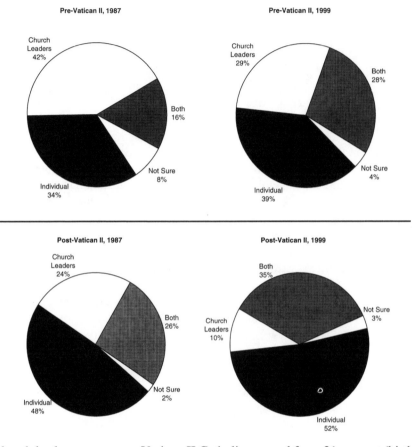

Pre-Vatican II, 1987

Pre-Vatican II, 1999

Post-Vatican II, 1987

Post-Vatican II, 1999

church leaders among pre–Vatican II Catholics ranged from 21 percent (birth control) to 37 percent (nonmarital sex); for the Catholics of Vatican II, the range was 13 percent to 27 percent; and among the youngest Catholics it was 6 percent to 14 percent.

Commitment to the Church and Locus of Moral Authority

We expected that Catholics who were most highly committed to the Church would be more likely than others to see church leaders as the proper source of moral teachings rather than to rely on their own consciences. Or to put it differently, they would be the most likely to have accepted church teachings on these matters in the formation of their consciences. Less committed Catholics would tend to emphasize individual conscience. This turned out to be true.

Table C.5.2 (appendix C) reports the patterns for high-commitment Catholics. Support for church leaders among Catholics of moderate and low commitment scores was very low. High-commitment Catholics looked more to church leaders than to their own consciences on four of the five issues; contraceptive birth control was the exception. Between 1987 and 1999, support for church leaders increased on two issues (remarriage and contraceptive birth control). In 1987 (figure 5.5), on three of the five issues (abortion, homosexuality, and nonmarital sex) more than half of the high-commitment Catholics said Catholics should look to church leaders alone. Across twelve years, the support level on each of those three issues dipped below half. However, support shifted not to the individual but to the "both" option. That is, the high-commitment Catholics who changed position said they thought these were issues on which the laity and hierarchy should work together. On abortion, homosexuality, and nonmarital sexual relations, the "both" option increased primarily from those who had previously supported church leaders. By 1999, then, more high-commitment Catholics looked either to dialogue with church leaders or to themselves alone rather than to church leaders alone. Nevertheless, strong support for church leaders persisted among the high-commitment Catholics. Why is this?

In chapter 2 we pointed out that during the twelve years of our study, regular weekend Mass attendance declined from 44 percent to 37 percent. There

Figure 5.5. Highly Committed Catholics Who Look to Church Leaders as the Locus of Moral Authority, 1987 and 1999 (in percent)

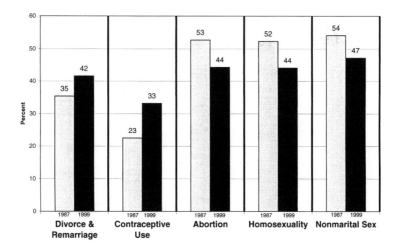

were similar declines in the percentage of Catholics saying the Church was among the most important influences in their lives (from 49 percent to 43 percent), and the percentage of those who said they would never leave the Church (from 64 percent to 57 percent). Thus it may be that the decline in the percentage of highly committed Catholics reflects the more frequent dropping out of Catholics who would look to conscience than to church leaders. If this is the case, as the high commitment core decreases in size, it will become more orthodox and conforming. This may be an important trend in coming years. This may be an important trend in coming years.

Level of Commitment Related to Gender and Generation

We have already seen (figure 5.1) a decline over time in the attribution of moral authority to church leaders when controlling for gender. Women have ceased to be the obedient Catholics of pre–Vatican II times. But as chapters 3 and 4 make clear, women still identify more closely than do men with being Catholic, they are more active in the sacramental life of the Church and they are more committed to it. Table 5.2 shows the relationship between high commitment, gender, and attitudes about the locus of moral authority in 1999. It makes clear that while women continued to be more highly committed to the Church than were men, they were significantly less likely than men to look to church leaders as the source for moral authority on the five issues under study. Almost half or more of the high-commitment men would look to church leaders on each of the five issues, including contraceptive birth control. Among the women, on only one issue (nonmarital sex) would as many as 40 percent look to church leaders as the locus of moral authority.

Which generation of Catholics in 1999 is the most committed to the Church

Table 5.2. Locus of Moral Authority on Five Issues, High-Commitment Catholics by Gender

Issue	Men %	Women %
Percentage of high-commitment Catholics who would look to Church leaders on		
Remarriage after divorce	49	36
Contraception	48	22
Abortion	55	37
Homosexuality	55	36
Nonmarital sex	56	40

Note: Twenty percent of the men and thirty percent of the women scored High on the Church Commitment Index.

as the source of moral authority? Table 5.3 shows the pattern. Most high-commitment Catholics are to be found in the older, not the younger, generation. Note the age structure of the Catholic population in the 1999 survey: post–Vatican II Catholics make up the largest segment (46 percent), with the Vatican II Catholics making up 34 percent. Only one in five Catholics are in the pre–Vatican II generation. The pre–Vatican generation is the most committed; by contrast, only 14 percent of the post–Vatican generation is highly committed. The Vatican II Catholics fall between the two.

More than half of the high-commitment pre–Vatican II Catholics would look to church leaders on four of the five issues; for Vatican II Catholics it was similar. However, among the 14 percent of the youngest high-commitment Catholics, never more than 27 percent (the figure on nonmarital sex) would look to church leaders as the voice of moral authority.

To sum up, young adult Catholics now make up about 46 percent of the Catholic adult population, but only one in seven identified themselves as highly committed to the Church. Only a minority of these young Catholics would look to church leaders as the source of moral authority in their lives. A little more than a fourth of Vatican II Catholics identified themselves as highly committed; about half of those continue to look to church leaders on most of these issues. One in five Catholics are in the pre–Vatican II generation (the most highly committed of the three), in which more than half continue to look to church leaders.

Average Level of Support for Church Leaders

Table 5.4 sums up our findings, using an index that presents a picture of the average level of support for church leaders for the five issues under study for

Table 5.3. Highly Committed Catholics Who Look to Church Leaders, by Generation, 1999

	Pre–Vatican II %	Vatican II %	Post–Vatican II %
Percent of total sample in each generation	20	34	46
Percent of each generation who are highly committed	40	27	14
Percent of highly committed who look to Church leaders on			
Remarriage after divorce	53	43	24
Contraception	42	34	19
Abortion	52	53	23
Homosexuality	52	49	26
Nonmarital Sex	57	53	27

Table 5.4.   Average Level of Support for Church Leaders on Five Issues of Sexual Morality

	Average Looking to Church Leaders (%)
Entire sample	20
Commitment level	
High	41
Medium	15
Low	6
Generation	
Pre–Vatican II (59 and older)	30
Vatican II (39 to 58)	24
Post–Vatican II (38 and younger)	12
Gender	
Men	23
Women	16

Note: The breakdowns by level of commitment, generation, and gender are all significant at .05.

1999. The numbers represent the percentage of people saying that moral authority is properly with church leaders, averaged across the five items.

In 1999, on average, one in five Catholics would look to church leaders as the locus of moral authority on the five issues under study. The sharpest differences occurred between high-commitment Catholics (41 percent) and low-commitment Catholics (6 percent). Generational differences ranked second in importance, with 30 percent of pre–Vatican II Catholics looking to church leaders as authorities, compared with only 12 percent of post–Vatican II Catholics. Gender differences, which are smallest, show that men (23 percent) were more likely to turn to church leaders than were women (16 percent).

Supporting Evidence from Other Research

Other recent studies agree with our findings on the changing locus of moral authority in the Catholic Church. For example, Lee and D'Antonio (2000) asked the following question in 1996:

> Which of the following options is closer to your personal belief about being a Roman Catholic? If you are unsure, please tell me that.
>
> 1. The pope is the authoritative voice speaking for Christ on earth. Roman Catholics must always obey the pope's formal teachings even when their own consciences may not be able to accept the pope's teaching.

2. The pope deserves respect and his teachings should be studied carefully. But ultimately, an individual should behave according to her/his conscience, even if it doesn't agree with the pope's teaching.
3. Unsure or don't know.

Seventy-one percent of the Catholics in the sample opted to follow conscience. *Among high-commitment Catholics,* half said they would follow their conscience and 42 percent said they would obey the pope, a sharp contrast with the 19 percent of the entire sample who said this.

Two other studies of generations of Catholics also depict a growing tendency for Catholics to stress individual conscience. Davidson et al. (1997) found that post–Vatican II Catholics were more willing than pre–Vatican II Catholics to disagree with Church teachings on sexual and reproductive issues. Also, a 1998 study of young Catholics (Dinges et al. 1998, 13–18) that included a large Latino subsample, reported that an overwhelming majority agreed that "in the realm of morality, the final authority about good and bad is the individual's informed conscience."

CONCLUSIONS

In this chapter we have presented findings that point to a growing disjuncture between the laity and the hierarchy on five central issues involving marriage and sexual morality. A growing majority of Catholics look to their own conscience, rather than to the magisterium, as the locus of moral authority. The trend has occurred in all three generations, and women are now more likely than men to rely on their own conscience. At the same time, the one in four Catholics who scored high on the Church Commitment Index were more likely than those who scored medium or low to look toward church leaders. On some items, half or more of the high-commitment Catholics would continue to look toward church leaders as the proper source of moral authority.

The trend over time suggests that the core of high-commitment Catholics (those who go to Mass regularly, who say they would never leave the Church, and who say the Church is among the most important influences on their lives) will continue to decline slowly toward the 20 percent level. That core will consist primarily of Vatican II Catholics and their parents; on issues of sexual morality, it will stand in stark contrast to the expanding majority of younger Catholics whose view on these matters reflects the Culture II progressivist orientation.

The evidence in this chapter strongly depicts a trend away from conformity and toward personal autonomy. Whether it reflects the growth of a superficial

Catholicism that Dulles and others fear from Culture II Catholics is a different matter. Rather, these findings add further support to the findings in chapter 3, namely, that Catholics distinguish between core features of their religion (the Sacraments, the Resurrection, the Real Presence), about which they look to the magisterium, and sexual issues that are more peripheral, about which they look more to their own conscience.

Chapter Six

Catholics and The Church's Social Teachings

Catholics assert that the Church's social teachings are an important part of their religion and identities. When asked, "How essential is each to your vision of what the Catholic faith is?" they ranked "charitable efforts toward helping the poor" among the top three of nineteen items. And when asked, "As a Catholic, how important is each of the following to you?" they ranked "Church involvement in activities directed toward social justice and helping the poor" third among six items. What do Catholics mean by these statements? This chapter examines the beliefs, attitudes, and behavior of American Catholics regarding the Church's teachings about the poor and also regarding specific teachings having to do with health care, nuclear weapons, the death penalty, and military funding.

VATICAN II: CALL TO MISSION

The Catholic Church's teachings are clear and forthright about its social vision. The writings of Pope Leo XIII are the modern source of the call for the Church to be active in public affairs and to strive for social action to ameliorate the human condition. Throughout the early part of the twentieth century, signs of increased engagement with the modern world were evident in the efforts of people like the Belgian priest (later Cardinal) Josef Cardign, who developed the Young Christian Students and Young Christian Workers movements and whose mantra "Observe, Judge, and Act" was brought to life in the United States in the Christian Family Movement, Young Christian Students, and labor movements. U.S. priests like John Ryan and George Higgins, as well as Catholic labor leaders like George Meany and Philip Murray, worked

hard for the rights of labor. The Democratic Party under the leadership of President Roosevelt received overwhelming Catholic voter support, resulting in
the establishment of Social Security and the passage of such pro-labor legislation as the Wagner Act in 1935. Activist editor Francis P. Lally called the
1930s "the first decade of widespread Catholic social consciousness in America" (Seidler and Meyer 1989, 43).

Vatican II validated such efforts in its call to action in the world for the laity.
Its *Decree on the Apostolate of Lay People* (>#5), exemplifies this call:

> Christ's redemptive work, while of itself directed toward the salvation of people,
> involves also the renewal of the whole temporal order. Hence the mission of the
> Church is not only to bring people the message and grace of Christ but also to pene-
> trate and perfect the temporal sphere.

The U.S. Catholic bishops, already active on many fronts in support of labor,
building hospitals, and starting schools, became strong supporters of a more
active lay apostolate. One way they did this was to issue statements such as
the following in 1976:

> Christian social teaching demands that citizens and public officials alike give serious
> consideration in all matters to the common good, to the welfare of society as a whole,
> which must be protected and promoted if individual rights are to be encouraged and
> upheld.[1]

More recently, in a statement on the one hundredth anniversary of Pope Leo
XIII's encyclical *Rerum Novarum,* the United States Catholic Conference
(USCC) outlined six basic principles (Administrative Board of the United
States Catholic Conference 1996, 13–14):

> In the Catholic social vision, the human person is central, the clearest reflection of God
> among us. Each person possesses a basic dignity that comes from God, not from any
> human quality or accomplishment, not from race or gender, age or economic status. . . .
>   Our dignity is protected when human rights are respected—the right to life and to
> those things which make life truly human: religious liberty, decent work, housing,
> health care, education, and the right to raise and provide for a family with dignity. . . .

---

1. In its statement on political responsibility, the Administrative Board of the United
States Catholic Conference (1976, 3) emphasized three issues in particular: (1) support for a constitutional amendment to restore the basic constitutional protection of the
right to life for the unborn child; (2) a decent income policy for those who cannot work
and adequate assistance to those in need, and opposition to efforts to eliminate or cur-
tail needed services and help; and (3) sufficient funding to make adequate education
available for all.

We realize our dignity and achieve our rights in relationship with others in our families and communities. No community is more central than the family—the basic cell of society.

Work is more than a way to make a living; it is a vocation, participation in creation. Workers have basic rights—to decent work, to just wages, to form and join unions, and to economic initiative, among others. . . .

People who are poor and vulnerable have a special place in Catholic teaching. The Scriptures tell us we will be judged by our response to the "least of these. . . ."

As Pope John Paul II reminds us, we are one human family despite differences of nationality or race; the poor are not a burden, but our sisters and brothers. Loving our neighbors has global dimensions in the 1990s.

In addition to statements of general principles, the bishops have issued very specific statements on legislation, often lobbying Congress. In the 1980s they issued two pastoral letters: one on nuclear war and peace, the other on the economy. The letters have provided a broad basis for their support of or opposition to particular bills. For example, they opposed many parts of the Welfare Reform statute of 1996, which nevertheless was passed by good margins in both houses. A growing number of bishops have also been active in the campaign against the death penalty. In May 2000, Cardinal Roger Mahoney of the Archdiocese of Los Angeles told the National Press Club that "recent calls for a moratorium on the death penalty signal the birth of a 'moral revolution' that may eventually lead to the end of the death penalty" (Eckstrom 2000).

To help them carry out their mission, the bishops have established the Office of Government Liaison to monitor legislation and occasionally to lobby. It publishes annual reports on legislation pending or completed, the relevance of the legislation to church teachings, government liaison actions in support or opposition, the impact of amendments, and (where relevant) voting records.

In 1969, the bishops founded the Catholic Campaign for Human Development, a nonprofit, anti-poverty social justice program. "Its mission is to address the root causes of poverty in America through promotion and support of community-controlled, self-help organizations and through transformative education" (CCHD 1998). The bishops founded it to promote "empowerment of the poor through a methodology of participation and education for justice, leading toward solidarity between poor and nonpoor as impelled by the Church's biblical tradition, modern Catholic social teaching, and the pervasive presence of poverty in the United States."

The grants and programs of the CCHD are supported by an annual collection in Catholic parishes. Of almost $14 million raised in 1997, three-fourths went to the national office; the other fourth remained in the local dioceses. In 1998, more than $11 million was allocated to more than three hundred projects nationwide, supporting community organizing, economic development, welfare-to-work programs, education, and public awareness. In addition to the national programs, statewide conferences operate under the bishops' auspices, engaging in a wide variety of ministries, including lobbying state legislatures pursuant to the church's teachings on matters under consideration.

The call for a more active engagement with the modern world has been heard and answered also by other organizations, including Catholic NET-WORK and the Center of Concern.

> NETWORK is a national Catholic social justice lobby founded in 1971 by 47 women religious. It is a nonprofit membership organization of lay and religious women and men who put their faith into action by lobbying to influence public policy in Washington. NETWORK's political lobbying goals are securing just access to economic resources, reordering federal budget priorities, and promoting global economic justice. (*Network Connection,* 1999)

NETWORK publishes a bimonthly newsletter highlighting major pieces of impending national legislation before Congress. Every year NETWORK evaluates the votes of all members of Congress on issues that the organization deems reflective of the Church's social teachings. NETWORK functions independently of the USCC Office of Government Liaison.

The Center of Concern, also organized in the 1970s and located in Washington, D.C., promotes social analysis, theological reflection, policy advocacy, and public education on issues of global development, human rights, and international finance. It publishes the bimonthly newsletter *Center Focus,* and like Catholic NETWORK, is supported by grants and donations from some thousands of friends nationwide.

These efforts have another purpose as well: they strive to raise the laity's awareness of its responsibility to work for the common good. This is no easy task in American society, especially as the strong strains of individual freedom and marketplace capitalism challenge attention to the common good.[2] James Hug, president of the Center of Concern, makes the point:

> To put it bluntly, Jesus came to bring Good News to the poor, freedom to captives, and recovery of sight to the blind; and to proclaim Jubilee (Luke 4.18–19). But Jubilee seems totally unrealistic in this 21st century globalizing world—if it was ever realistic anywhere. We who have been entrusted with Jesus' mission here and now have a serious challenge of discernment and careful inculturation. Otherwise, the heart of

---

2. See Bellah et al. (1985). Greeley (1989) reported that despite the strong strains of personal autonomy, Catholics continue to exhibit more concern for community and the public good than do Protestants. The same thesis is found in Douglass and Hollenbach (1994).

Jesus' message is at risk of being reduced to personalistic and spiritualized applications–subordinated to or domesticated by the dominant American culture. (Hug 1999)

Social Teachings and the Laity's Response

Since the days of the New Deal, American Catholics have been generally supportive of labor, health care, and family issues associated with proactive government programs. Yet in the 1980s, President Ronald Reagan attracted a large number of so-called Reagan Democrats after more and more Catholics had moved out of ghettos and into more affluent suburban areas. The pastoral letters written during the Reagan years by the bishops on nuclear war and peace (1983) and on the U.S. economy (1986) indicated the hierarchy's willingness to address controversial political issues in addition to abortion and reproductive ethics. Our research shows trends in the laity's attitudes on these issues.

Our first survey was in 1987, just a year after the publication of the U.S. Bishops' pastoral letter on the U.S. economy, *Economic Justice for All,* and three years after the pastoral letter on the arms race, *Nuclear War and Peace.* We probed the laity's knowledge about and support for the bishops' teachings. In 1993, we repeated the questions about the bishops' two pastoral letters, and in 1999 we asked a five-item question about social and political issues related to the pastoral letters and to other issues. Also in all three surveys we included questions about the qualities of "being a good Catholic," including one item about donating time or money to help the poor.

The Bishops' Pastoral Letters: A Retrospective

In 1983, the American Catholic bishops published a pastoral letter expressing their opposition to the continuing arms buildup and the use of nuclear weapons. It outlined "universal principles" and called for immediate bilateral agreements to halt the testing, production, and deployment of new nuclear weapons systems. Three years later the bishops issued another pastoral letter, this time questioning some of the nation's economic policies and calling for more economic justice. The prelates went on to declare that "all economic decisions must be judged in light of what they do for the poor, what they do to the poor, and what they enable the poor to do for themselves."

The letters were designed to stimulate debate in the public arena, and they did so. The national media gave them extraordinary coverage, and critics such as Michael Novak insisted on modifications to the documents, which they considered unfair attacks on U.S. nuclear defense efforts and capitalist policies. How broadly were these letters known by Catholics?

In 1987, 29 percent of respondents had heard about or read the peace pastoral, and 25 percent the pastoral on the economy. Business leaders, executives, and professionals, Catholic college graduates, and regular Mass attenders more than other Catholics had some familiarity with them. Among those who knew about the pastorals, 57 percent were in overall agreement with the thrust of the peace pastoral, while 71 percent supported the economy pastoral (D'Antonio et al. 1989, 170–71). In sum, the letters were supported by the minority of Catholics who knew about them. Although the letters were seen as appropriate activities of the bishops, there was no evidence of their having any effect on laity behavior. Catholics continued to give Reagan their support in the 1984 elections, despite his known opposition to the substance of the peace pastoral.

In the 1993 survey only 18 percent of American Catholics said they had heard about or read the peace pastoral and 19 percent, the economy pastoral. The pastorals apparently had faded into history. Still, the bishops continued to issue formal statements emphasizing the need to reach out to the poor, to provide jobs with living wages, to provide basic health care for all, and to seek reductions in nuclear arms. How closely do the laity's attitudes reflect specific items from the bishops' agenda?

The Poor and Being a Good Catholic

Living the Gospel entails more than knowing the bishops' pastorals or having attitudes that correspond to the Church's teachings. It includes action, as one Catholic involved in a small faith community told us:

> Living the Gospel—that's the challenge! And that was one of the goals of our small community that we never really achieved. Because I'm really interested in social concerns, I tried to get people to go to the homeless shelter with me, but they don't want to do that. (Lee and D'Antonio 2000, 161)

The question arises, what kind of action? Action that criticizes the existing society? Action that aids individual poor people or improves the lot of all the poor in society? Action that challenges our business-as-usual American way of life? Leege (1986) reported that only about half of Catholic parishes sponsor outreach programs of a charitable nature, and even fewer (only about a quarter) attempt to address important social issues. Perhaps reflecting the opportunities that are available to them in their parishes, Catholics are more ready to do acts of charity and help individual poor people than to engage in actions critical of social policies. All research shows this.[3] Our surveys asked only one question about such acts of charity (giving time or money to help the poor) and found in

---

3. See for example, Gremillion and Castelli (1987); Hoge (1976); and Davidson, Mock, and Johnson (1997).

all three that roughly half believed that one could be a good Catholic and still not do such acts of charity (table 6.1). Moreover, the trend has clearly been away from the idea that acts of charity are requisites of being a good Catholic. This trend may be a part of the times: most public opinion polls show ambivalent attitudes toward the poor. Americans are willing to help the truly needy[4] but have grown increasingly suspicious of welfare programs, with anecdotes of welfare abuse dominating the public debates.[5] In 1995–96, Congress passed legislation, with the broad support of the public, ending the decades of social welfare that the bishops had lobbied strongly to reform but not dismantle. This pattern seems consistent with the finding that 53 percent of Americans said that welfare cuts meant that the government "was ending a system that has kept poor people in poverty;" only 30 percent said "the government was giving up its proper role of helping poor people" (*The Public Perspective* 1998, 35).

The finding that helping the poor is perceived less and less as necessary for a good Catholic was further supported by data from a 1996 nationwide survey (Lee and D'Antonio, 2000), in which 58 percent of all Catholics agreed that one could be a good Catholic without helping the poor. These responses seem to contradict the high rank Catholics give to "charitable efforts and church involvement in activities toward helping the poor" (in chapter 3).

A possible interpretation is that Catholics accept the general principle of caring for others and agree with the principle of helping the poor, but do not see these principles as having the same level of importance as beliefs about the Resurrection and the Real Presence of Christ in the Eucharist. They may feel that core beliefs like the Resurrection are required for being a good Catholic, but may be less inclined to believe that helping the poor is an obligation. They may be more inclined to see concern for others as a personal, voluntary expression of their faith. This was the case with the late William Simon, the conservative financier, businessman, and philanthropist, who served as secretary of the treasury in the Reagan administration. He personally tended to the ill and destitute, including patients with AIDS. He told the *Chronicle of Philanthropy*

---

4. A 1997 Survey for the National Commission on Philanthropy and Civic Renewal reported that 68 percent of Americans said they had donated time or money to help people in need, such as the poor, hungry, or homeless. Cited in *The Public Perspective,* February/March 1998, 24.

5. A series of national surveys between 1992 and 1997 assessed American attitudes toward the poor. Between 45 percent and 53 percent said that "the poor people have it easy today because they can get government benefits without having to do anything in return." On the other hand, between 39 percent and 49 percent said "Poor people have hard lives because government benefits don't go far enough for them to live decently" (*The Public Perspective* 1998, 34).

Table 6.1.   Catholics Who Said You Can Be a Good Catholic without Donating Time or Money to Help the Poor, 1987, 1993, and 1999

	1987 %	1993 %	1999 %
You can be a good Catholic without donating time or money to help the poor. Agree.	46	52	56

two years before he died that "writing checks for charities is necessary and important, but it can't compare with corporal works of mercy, which are infinitely greater. My Eucharistic ministry is the most important thing I do and have ever done" (Obituary 2000).

Gender, Generation, and Commitment

Do men and women differ? What about Gen X Catholics compared with the baby boomers of Vatican II and the pre–Vatican II Catholics who grew up during the Great Depression? In table 6.2 we apply the controls for gender, generation, and degree of commitment to the Church, and here we find some modification in the general finding, yet the trend continues (see also figure 6.1). Women have been consistently more likely than men to view helping the poor as an important part of what it means to be a good Catholic. Still, the trend over time has been a 10-point decline among both men and women in this belief.

Post–Vatican II Catholics were most likely to say you can be a good Catholic without donating time or money to help the poor; by 1999, 6 out of 10 held that attitude. The Vatican II baby boomers remained the most stable over time, with less than half supporting the attitude that you can be a good Catholic without helping the poor. A majority of pre–Vatican II Catholics did not see the importance to their faith of helping the poor.

Highly committed Catholics provided the strongest support for the importance of helping the poor, but their level of support declined by 10 percentage points over time. Catholics whose commitment to the Church was low were the most likely to say that helping the poor was not necessary.

Catholics' Attitudes on Social and Political Issues

In the 1999 survey we included five items on social issues that the bishops have spoken out on. The bishops have been strongly supportive of health care for the poor, elimination of the death penalty, reduction of nuclear weapons, and reduction of funds for the military. They have also opposed further welfare

Table 6.2. Catholics Who Said You Can Be a Good Catholic without Donating Time or Money to Help the Poor, Controlling for Gender, Generations, and Commitment

	1987 %	1993 %	1999 %
Gender			
Men	50	59	61
Women	43	50	53
Generation			
Pre–Vatican II	47	58	55
Vatican II	46	45	48
Post–Vatican II	47	61	63
Commitment to the Church			
High	40	47	50
Medium	48	55	56
Low	51	61	69

Figure 6.1

Catholics Who agreed "You can be a Good Catholic without Donating Time or Money to Help the Poor," by Gender, Generation, and Commitment, 1999

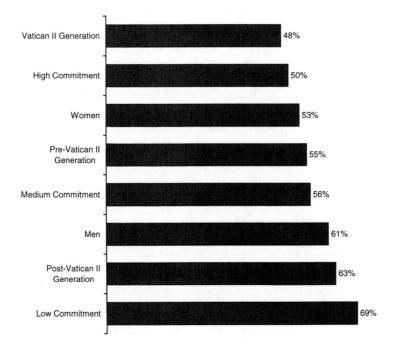

program cuts. On three of the five items, the laity were clearly aligned with the bishops (table 6.3). For example, three out of four Catholics strongly agreed that more money should be provided for health care for poor children. But only one in three strongly supported more funds for the military, and only one in five further cuts in welfare programs. However, on the death penalty and on nuclear arms reduction, they were of a mixed mind: More than half strongly agreed that there should be stricter enforcement of the death penalty, while they were split evenly regarding further reduction of nuclear weapons.

Table 6.3 also shows the effect of gender on these five issues, while tables 6.4 and 6.5 show the impact of generation and level of commitment to the Church. While both men and women were strongly supportive of more money for health care, the women were much more supportive than the men. Men and women agreed on welfare programs. More men than women wanted stricter enforcement of the death penalty, while the two were evenly split on the desire to reduce nuclear arms. Men were somewhat more likely than women to support more funds for the military. In sum, insofar as there were differences in gender, women were somewhat closer than the men to the position taken by the bishops on these issues. In the past ten years, a growing number of Catholic leaders have called for an end to the death penalty. Pope John Paul II, the U.S. Catholic bishops, and Sister Helen Prejean with her own personal story have led a growing debate in the public arena. Since 1976, when the death penalty was reinstated in the United States, most polls have shown about 70 to 75 percent of Americans favor it. Catholics have been as strong in their support of the death penalty as other Americans. For example, Gallup (1999, 114–15) reported that 77 percent of the American population overall, and 75 percent of those who said that religion was very important to them, supported the death penalty.

Table 6.4 compares the attitudes of the three generations on the five issues. There was broad support in all three generations for more health care for poor children. Pre–Vatican II Catholics were more likely than younger generations to strongly favor stiffer enforcement of the death penalty. There was little difference among the generations regarding nuclear arms reductions and cutbacks

Table 6.3. Catholics Who Said They Strongly Agreed with Five Social and Political Issues, by Gender, 1999

Issue	Entire Sample %	Men %	Women %
More money for health care for poor children	73	66	80
Stiffer enforcement of death penalty	54	59	51
Nuclear arms reduction	50	51	52
More funds for the military	32	37	31
More cutbacks in welfare programs	22	25	22

in welfare programs. But the same does not hold for funds to the military, where Pre–Vatican II Catholics significantly differed from the other two generations in their strong support for the military. On these issues, the oldest generation of Catholics deviated the most from the Church's social teachings. On the desire to reduce nuclear arms, the generations were in general agreement. Given the tendency of pro-military groups to oppose any further reductions in nuclear weapons, this finding suggests that the bishops' call for reductions in nuclear arms may have found some resonance among America's Catholics.

Do highly committed Catholics differ from other Catholics on these five social issues? The findings are mixed (see table 6.5). All groups were support-ive of providing more money for health care for the poor and opposed to more cutbacks in welfare programs. Highly committed Catholics gave less support to stiffer enforcement of the death penalty than did other Catholics. At the same time, the highly committed Catholics were more strongly in favor of providing more funds to the military and less in favor of nuclear arms reduction.

Overall, on these issues, there is broad support for the Church's teachings, whatever the person's level of commitment to the Church itself. When we compare these findings with the earlier findings on the relationship between being a good Catholic and donating time or money to help the poor, we may get a better understanding of Catholics. They accept the importance of the teachings, but are no longer sure government is the appropriate agent to carry them out. The teachings may not imply to them that they have a personal responsibility. Support for this interpretation is found in the Catholic vote in national elections over the years. Catholics have given strong support to New Deal legislation, to such health care programs as Medicare and Medicaid, and to the environment and education. This was especially apparent in the 1996 elections (White and D'Antonio 1997). This interpretation fits well with the

Table 6.4. Catholics Who Said They Strongly Agreed with Five Social and Political Issues, by Generation, 1999

Issue	Entire Sample %	Pre– Vatican II %	Vatican II %	Post– Vatican II %
More money for health care for poor children	73	73	72	75
Stiffer enforcement of death penalty	54	60	54	54
Nuclear arms reduction	50	51	47	54
More funds for the military	32	55	31	27
More cutbacks in welfare programs	22	20	22	27

Table 6.5. Catholics Who Said They Strongly Agreed with Five Social and Political
Issues, by Level of Church Commitment, 1999

	Total %	High Commitment %	Medium Commitment %	Low Commitment %
More money for health care	73	71	74	74
Stiffer enforcement of death penalty	55	48	56	61
Nuclear arms reduction	51	48	51	57
More funds for military	34	39	35	24
More cutbacks in welfare reform	24	19	27	17

headlines from an article on a *New York Times* Poll of New York area
Catholics in December 1999. It stated that New York Catholics were looking
for a leader to succeed Cardinal O'Connor "who will tackle poverty and home-
lessness as priorities of the Church" (Schemo 1999).

CONCLUSIONS

Catholics affirm that concern for the poor is an important part of their identity as
Catholics. However, there was a slippage of 10 percentage points in the number
of Catholics saying this over the 12 years of our study. The gender, generation,
and commitment variables had only modest impact on the general findings. Even
among those Catholics with the highest commitment to the Church, half of them
said that you can be a good Catholic without donating time or money to help the
poor. That attitude increased by 10 percentage points in 12 years.

The Catholic Church has stated clear principles about the responsibility of
Catholics to bring about a more just social order, one that respects human life
from conception to death. In chapter 5 we found that on certain key moral
issues, the laity had moved steadily away from conformity to church teachings. Their attitude was that the locus of moral authority should rest with themselves as responsible individuals. This movement toward autonomy was
apparent also in the findings reported in this chapter. It is not that the laity no
longer conform to the Church's teachings on matters of social justice, but more
likely that they do not see active pursuit of social justice as one of their responsibilities. They express the concern for the poor that has long been a characteristic of Catholics. But doing something concrete seems more like an option
than an expectation of a responsible Catholic. To the extent that the laity see
social concern for the poor as no more than an option, it may be another sign

of the difficulty the church leaders have today in developing the consistent life ethic as part of the Catholic community's sense of being.

In an April 2000 convocation in New York City, Bishop Kenneth E. Untener of Saginaw, Michigan, suggested that "Catholics deserved only a 'D' grade for their record in trying to change structures and policies that we think are unfair" (Briefs, *National Catholic Reporter,* 28 April 2000, 8). Untener gave Catholics "an A-plus on helping their own family and neighbors, and said their performance was also good on contributing to causes such as relief for disaster areas. But Catholics have not done as well on moving from charity to analyzing and addressing the causes of the human need they see in the world."

The report continued: "The bishop appealed for efforts to teach basic principles of Catholic social teaching to all members of the church, and to help them see its connection to the Bible, church tradition and spirituality." The article concluded with the announcement by "George B. Horton, director of social and community development for the New York archdiocese, that the archdiocese planned to start 10 small groups of people who would receive training in Catholic social teaching and help each other to conduct 'public discipleship' activities."

The findings in this chapter make clear that much effort will have to be put forth if any significant changes are to be forthcoming from this new initiative. We have seen that Catholics affirm in principle the church's commitment to reach out to the poor and needy, but do not necessarily perceive this affirmation to require them to do something personally. As on questions of sexual morality, to date the influence of the bishops on these social issues has been modest.[6]

---

6. See also Leege and Mueller, 2000. They analyze a broad array of data for the period 1952–1996, and suggest that "perhaps the research agenda of the future will be to map the ways Catholic charitable acts in this more conservative and self-centered generation lead to systemic betterment of society" (26).

Chapter Seven

Priest Shortages and Accommodations in Ministry

In June 2000, the U.S. National Conference of Catholic Bishops (NCCB) met in Milwaukee to consider the findings of the two-year study it had commissioned, "Impact of Fewer Priests on the Pastoral Ministry." The meeting was the first where the bishops publicly discussed the priest shortage and considered ways of dealing with it. The study points out that the average age of priests has continued to rise; fifty-seven years for diocesan priests, and sixty-three for religious. The ratio of priests to Catholics is growing at an alarming rate: 1:1,257 overall[1] and higher in the West (1:1,752), an area of rapid and ethnically diverse growth. More disturbing, if the ratio takes into account only priests active in parishes rather than the total priest population, it is 1:2,185. The aging and retirement of priests can only exacerbate the ratio in the future.

The study also describes a shortage of replacements. In 2000, about 3,500 candidates were in graduate-level seminaries, less than half the number in 1965. Major archdioceses like Boston, New York, Chicago, and Los Angeles ordained fewer than ten men each (Osting 2000). Archbishop Theodore McCarrick reported about twelve ordinations per year in his diocese of Newark, New Jersey, where there are 544 priests and about 200 deaths and retirements expected to occur shortly. Twenty years from now, the Newark diocese expects to have about only one-third as many priests. Although 13,000 ordained deacons work in ministries either full- or part-time, they sim-

---

1. This ratio (1:1,257) differs somewhat from our calculations in table 1.3 (1:1,330 in 1999), which were based on figures from the *Official Catholic Directory*. Because we are discussing findings from the bishops' survey here, we used its figure; the difference between the two is not large.

ply do not absorb the slack because there are 20 percent fewer priests and nearly a third more parishioners than in 1965.

Findings such as these were disseminated promptly through the press, both secular and Catholic, as were the reactions and concerns of bishops and other NCCB participants. Auxiliary Bishop Thomas Curry of Los Angeles, reporting that immigration had increased some parishes in his archdiocese to eighteen thousand households, wondered about the Church's emphasis on reaching out to dormant Catholics. "If we invite (them) back, what in heaven's name will we do with them?" (McClory 2000).

Consequences of the priest shortage are apparent in dioceses and parishes, according to the U.S. bishops' study. Forty-two percent of dioceses have reduced the number of Sunday Masses. More than a quarter of parishes lack a full-time priest. Thirteen percent of dioceses are closing parishes, though for more reasons than a decline in clergy. Eighty-three percent of dioceses reported that they have fewer priests than needed. Although the only functions limited to priests are celebrating Mass and absolving sin, Catholics customarily want priests to preside at weddings, funerals, baptisms, and other parish functions (Osting 2000). In addition to the problems of staffing, there are problems of stress, exhaustion, isolation, and low morale that ordained ministers experience.

How does the Catholic laity view this situation? According to one commentator at the bishops' conference, "It's true that the best kept secret is the shortage of priests. We have kept it from the laity. We have covered it up in every way imaginable and pretend it doesn't exist" (McClory 2000). Perhaps some Catholics don't know the magnitude of the shortage, but the national poll of 2,600 Catholics commissioned by the bishops found that 74 percent of lay Catholics were aware of the dwindling number of priests.

This chapter examines the reactions of the laity to the growing priest shortage over a twelve-year period, 1987–99. As background, we trace the history of the declining priesthood starting with the years following Vatican II. Then, through data from our surveys, we discuss the laity's views since 1987 on the services desired from priests and the accommodations that would be acceptable to keep ministry accessible.

Decreasing Clergy since Vatican II

The Catholic population in the United States has grown enormously since colonial times. Just between 1960 and 1999, the increase in real numbers was substantial: 42 million became 62 million even though the Catholic percentage of the U.S. population remained at about 23 percent.

By the late 1960s, resignations of clergy had become a new problem.

Whereas about 0.1 percent of diocesan priests resigned annually in the 1940s and 1950s, the percentage increased twentyfold by 1969 (NORC 1972, 277; Schoenherr and Greeley 1974, 408). Overall, an estimated 10 percent of clergy left between 1966 and 1972 (Schoenherr and Sorensen 1982). For a period of time, net losses appeared smaller, probably because of replacement by newly ordained priests, postponed retirements, and other factors. For example, Fichter (1974, 22) noted a net loss of only 2.5 percent, from 59,892 priests in 1967 to 57,431 in 1972. However, the numbers of diocesan seminary students dropped dramatically, from 26,200 in 1966 to 13,600 in 1972. A combination of high resignation rates and low replacement rates produced a net loss of U.S. priests of about 14 percent; 59,000 in 1966 decreased to 51,000 by 1978.

The clergy decline was even greater if priests belonging to religious orders were included. Resignation rates for them were higher than those for diocesan priests. The reduction in total church professionals from 1966 to 1972 was 15.3 percent, according to official Church statistics (Fichter 1974, 21).

In 1993, Schoenherr and Young published a detailed demographic analysis of the diocesan priests and made predictions about the growing priest shortage in their book *Full Pews and Empty Altars: Demographics of the Priest Shortage in United States Catholic Dioceses.* Whereas in 1966 there had been one diocesan priest for every 1,100 parishioners, Schoenherr and Young predicted that by 2005 there would be one for every 2200.[2] In a 1998 update in *Sociology of Religion,* Young noted that "projections for the year 2015 show that the total decline in the clergy population since 1966 is likely to reach somewhere between thirty-eight percent under optimistic conditions and sixty-one percent under pessimistic conditions" (1998, 15).

From the 1970s on, sociologists and others have scrutinized the sources of priest resignations. Some examined how the structure of ecclesiastical Catholicism, the social psychological characteristics of clergy, and the organizational environment of priestly life affected priests' commitment to clerical life. (See Cozzens 2000; Hall and Schneider 1973; Kennedy and Heckler 1972; Schallert and Kelley 1970; Seidler 1979.) Others anticipated the consequences of priest resignations, most important, the institutional crisis induced by resignations combined with seminary losses (Fichter 1974; Hoge 1987). Seidler (1974) and Greeley (1977) noted the tendency of American bishops to overlook the crisis and proceed with traditional approaches. Young (1998) and Wallace (1992) pointed out that a larger priest to parishioner ratio implied less priestly influence over the spiritual lives and doctrinal understanding of individual Catholics.

---

2. These figures are different from those in chapter 1, because those figures include both diocesan and religious-order priests.

Young also commented on potential changes in the political and economic structures of the Church and speculated that some combination of sacrament, priesthood, centralized control, compulsory celibacy, and male exclusivity would be weakened.

Some authors focused on consequences that would open up ministry to formerly excluded groups; others discussed the potential for reducing services usually provided by priests, for spreading existing clergy more thinly over geographical territories, for closing parishes, and the like. In fact, there has been both expansion and truncation of ministry. Ecclesiastical labor has been stretched by involving the laity more in ministry and administration of parishes and dioceses. At the same time, particularly in rural areas, the shortage of priests has led in some cases to importing missionaries from foreign countries such as Poland and Ireland.

Strategies to Increase the Church's Workforce

The clergy shortage called for some strategies to increase the workforce of the Church in the United States. A visible strategy was the expansion of women's roles. Vatican II's documents on the laity's ministry and on worship encouraged both men and women to increase their involvement. Other Council documents provided for women's appointment as diocesan chancellors, auditors, assessors, defenders of the marriage bond, promoters of justice, and judges on diocesan courts. As Howard (1999) observed, Vatican Council II theologically legitimated women's increased assumption of leadership positions, and the priest shortage created new opportunities.

The U.S. hierarchy has been slow to implement the reforms of Vatican II regarding women, and implementation has varied across dioceses. Yet, an increasing number of parishes are headed by women administrators, and large numbers of women attend national Church conferences, head up diocesan ministries, and serve on parish councils. Murnion (1992) and Murnion and DeLambo (1999) reported that the post-Vatican II burgeoning lay ministry comprised largely women. As noted in chapter 1, Murnion and DeLambo found that the vast majority of the 30,000 lay ministers in parish and diocesan offices are women. Although women continue to be marginal to decision making, they have increased their influence, especially in parish life. And there is evidence that they are filling gaps in ministry created by a declining priesthood.

Drawing data from *The Official Catholic Directory,* the Summer 1999 *CARA Report* (from the Center for Applied Research in the Apostolate) documented a trend in local congregations without a resident pastor. In 1965, there were 549; in 1985, 1,051, and by 1997, 2,319. Froehle and Gautier (2000), using CARA data, reported similar but slightly different figures and noted that there were nearly 2,500 parishes with no resident pastor at present. Wallace (1992) found that both women religious and laywomen headed a large percentage of parishes not administered by a resident priest. In short, as the laity assumed more ministerial roles, women were at the forefront. This apparently met with widespread approval. In our 1999 survey, 81 percent of the laity favored women as lectors and 76 percent as Eucharistic ministers. Further, 66 percent approved of ordaining women as deacons, and more than half, as priests.

Another visible strategy was the increasing ordination of male deacons. Their number grew threefold between 1980 and 1999. However, the permanent diaconate, established by Vatican II, has met with problems that affect deacons themselves and also their relationships with priests and laypeople. DeRego and Davidson (1998) describe the role conflict and ambiguity experienced by deacons who find both satisfaction and frustration in their positions. They also point out that having deacons (as well as laymen and laywomen) assume some of the responsibilities formerly reserved to priests does not address the centrality of priests to the administration of the Church and the sacraments. Deacons cannot perform certain sacramental functions; priests remain the lynchpin for the functioning of the Church. Further, laypeople tend to view deacons as "underqualified priests or overqualified laity," according to a 1996 national study on the permanent diaconate in the United States, commissioned by the U.S. Conference of Catholic Bishops. They simply want priests to provide certain ministries and fill roles in parishes and dioceses.

As a consequence of the controversy over deacons, some bishops have stopped ordaining them. Other Church leaders want changes, such as a review of ordination, clarification of priests' and deacons' liturgical roles, and improved training in preaching (Rice 1997). Meanwhile, the problem of a priest shortage and the need for an enlarged workforce have grown.

We next examine the laity's views toward clergy shortages. We report findings for two possible responses to the growing priest shortage: scaling down services and expanding the population eligible for ordination.

Scaling Down Services

Starting in 1967, the peak year of the first exodus of men from the priesthood, the clergy shortage in the United States made possible a range of creative solutions. Laypeople became involved as representatives, experts, and specialists in parish administration and ministry in various parts of the United States, depending on diocesan conditions and the leadership style of the bishop. Assuming that the current boundaries of priesthood will remain early in the twenty-first century, we expect that such adaptations will be further employed or there will be a reduction of priestly services.

In both the 1993 and 1999 surveys, we asked respondents about their willingness to accommodate to changes in running parishes and in supplying pastoral services. Data from Dean Hoge's (1987) *The Future of Catholic Leadership: Responses to the Priest Shortage* provided the statistics for 1985 so that trends for the entire sample could be examined at three points in time. The data showed a mixed pattern of willingness to implement changes in parish life and ministry. Some modifications were more acceptable in 1999 than they were in 1985; others became less satisfactory.

We asked respondents, "If shortages made it necessary, how willing would you be to have parishes administered by a layperson and visiting priest rather than a resident priest?" (See Table 7.1.) Over time, the percentage of Catholics accepting this increased: in 1985, 39 percent thought a lay administrator and visiting priest would be satisfactory; by 1993, 56 percent thought so; in 1999, the percentage dropped to 51. In the 1990s, the laity was split about 50–50 on the need for a resident priest.

We also asked respondents if a communion service led by a layperson would be acceptable. Although less than 20 percent approved of that on a regular basis, 68 percent agreed that it was satisfactory on occasion. In sum, about half of the laity was amenable to running parishes differently in at least certain respects.

Even though the trend was toward increased acceptance of cutbacks in pastoral services, a majority of respondents in all three surveys remained unwilling to accept these changes. In 1985, only 28 percent agreed that having fewer than one Mass a week was acceptable; in both 1993 and 1999, 41 percent concurred. Still, about 60 percent did not. Respondents were asked if not having a priest to visit the sick or to administer the last rites were satisfactory options.

Table 7.1.   Laity's Acceptance of Changes in Parish Administration and Pastoral Services, 1985, 1993, and 1999

	1985 %	1993 %	1999 %
No resident priest: only lay administrator and visiting priest	39	56	51
Communion service led regularly or occasionally by a layperson	*	*	68
Fewer than one Mass a week	28	41	41
No priest to visit the sick	24	41	34
No priest for last rites	15	30	20

* Not asked

In 1985, only 24 percent agreed that having no priest to visit the sick was permissible. By 1993, 41 percent found it satisfactory, but by 1999 the percentage had dropped to 34 percent. Stated in a different way, in the 1990s, between 60 and 65 percent thought having a priest to visit the sick was important. About 80 percent wanted priests to administer the last rites too, though there was some fluctuation in 1993. In general, the 1999 data showed the laity to be much less agreeable to reducing ministry to the sick and dying than it had been.

Overall, the laity endorsed changes in parish management more than it supported any reduction in the pastoral services priests typically perform. As we will discuss in chapter 8, we found strong support for lay involvement in deciding local parish issues, such as budget expenditures and priest selection. By 1999, 60 percent or more of the respondents, regardless of gender, generation, or level of commitment, wanted more participation in administering parishes.

We cross-tabulated our three key variables (gender, generation, and commitment) with the laity's views on reducing services that priests typically perform, using data from 1985 to 1999. There were some differences by gender. From 1993 to 1999, men's attitudes remained stationary except that men became more eager to have priests for the last rites. Women became significantly less agreeable to cutting back any services except having fewer Masses per week.

Regarding generations, the pre-Vatican II and the post-Vatican II generations mostly maintained their views between 1993 and 1999, with one exception each (see Table 7.2). The youngest generation wanted priests for the last rites and the oldest generation favored having them visit the sick more in 1999 than in 1993. However, it is important to note that the oldest generation was at least as accepting of change on all issues as the other generations were. Any suppositions that pre-Vatican II Catholics are more conservative across the board are simply unfounded.

Over time, the Vatican II generation became less accepting of not having priests to visit the sick, administer the last rites, and run parishes. We do not have a clear explanation for that. Potential explanations run the gamut from this generation's personal concerns about having ministers available to them to their impatience with the decreasing clergy problem. This pattern for the Vatican II generation could also be a life-cycle effect or evidence of fluctuations in their thinking about the clergy shortage. Like the other generations, about 60 percent of the Vatican II generation was not supportive of having fewer Masses.

We looked to see if people highly committed to the Church had attitudes about priestly services different from those of other Catholics. The analysis showed that their responses were not very different from the entire sample's as shown in table 7.1. Combining the "somewhat acceptable" responses with the "very acceptable" ones, by 1999 about half of the highly committed were

Table 7.2. Laity's Acceptance of Decreasing Priestly Ministry, by Generation, 1993 and 1999

	Mass Less Than Once a Week		No Priest to Visit the Sick		No Priest for Last Rites		No Resident Priest	
	1993 (%)	1999 (%)	1993 (%)	1999 (%)	1993 (%)	1999 (%)	1993 (%)	1999 (%)
Post–Vatican II	41	41	34	31	27	20	56	55
Vatican II	43	43	45	33	31	14	59	48
Pre–Vatican II	41	39	56	43	36	32	57	54

accepting of not having a resident priest; 35 percent were accepting of fewer Masses; 40 percent and 22 percent, respectively, were accepting of not having a priest to visit the sick or to administer the last rites.

Expanding Ordination?

Reporting about the *New York Times* poll of Catholics in the New York region, Schemo (1999) noted that respondents recognized that the numbers of priests had been dwindling, and they were receptive to envisioning changed parishes in the future. When asked about the most important problems facing the Church, New Yorkers identified the shortage of priests as second; poverty was first. In our surveys of 1993 and 1999, as well as in Hoge's 1985 survey, we found that Catholics were willing to expand the definition of *priest* beyond its current boundaries—a policy that would maintain the services of priests. Those responding to the *Times* telephone poll agreed: they favored "modernizing and opening up the Church by allowing priests to marry and ordaining women as priests."

We explored the issue of expanding ordination to groups other than celibate males. In all three surveys, respondents were asked if it would be a good thing to allow married men to be ordained. Support grew from 63 percent in the 1987 survey to 72 percent by 1993 and remained steady at 71 percent in 1999 (see table 7.3). In 1999, we probed further by asking if it were a good idea for priests who had married to be returned to active ministry; 77 percent of respondents agreed.

Regarding the ordination of women, table 7.3 shows data from Gallup polls across twenty-five years that indicated increasing approval over time. In 1974, only 29 percent thought it was a good idea. Consent had increased to 40 percent by the end of the 1970s and continued to increase during the 1980s to half of the respondents by 1985. Eight years later, our 1993 survey showed a dramatic jump to 64 percent. In the 1999 survey, we divided the question of

Table 7.3 Laity's Acceptance of Clergy Expansion, 1974–99

	1974 (%)	1979 (%)	1985 (%)	1987 (%)	1993 (%)	1999 (%)
Ordination of married men				63	72	71
Married priests returned to active ministry						77
Ordination of women	29	40	50		64	
Ordination of celibate women						62
Ordination of married women						53

Source: Gallup Organization

ordaining women into married and celibate women; 62 percent approved ordaining celibate women; 53 percent, married women.

In sum, respondents favored expanding ordination to married men and women at an increasing level over time. By 1999, approval ranged from 53 percent for married women to 77 percent for formerly active priests. Do subgroups have different attitudes regarding ordination? In this longitudinal study, we paid particular attention to the variables that were most predictive for all the issues treated; namely, gender, commitment, and generation. In this chapter our analyses of the data explored thirty-one categories of respondents. We present findings from sixteen subgroups in table 7.4, which shows support for expanding ordination in most of them; it also addresses the issue of who opposes opening up ordination to the priesthood.

Catholics in all categories agreed that priests who had married should be allowed to return to active ministry. Levels of support ranged from 70 percent to 89 percent. At least 65 percent also approved the ordination of married men; approval across subgroups ranged between 65 percent and 79 percent. Several categories of respondents fell below 65 percent but were still noticeably above 50 percent approval: they included people who had thirteen or more years of Catholic schooling (55 percent) and those who were highly committed (57 percent). In short, respondents were positive about having married men (previously ordained or not) as their ministers.

More than half of respondents in all subgroups (ranging from 55 percent to 72 percent) concurred with ordaining celibate women. Subgroups that fell below a 55 percent approval rate included those educated in Catholic schools beyond high school (51 percent), the highly committed (42 percent), and the oldest generation (49 percent). It is important to note that there is correlation between number of years of Catholic schooling and level of commitment, but it is not strong. That is, many highly committed Catholics were not educated in Catholic colleges.

Finally, all but five subgroups approved of the ordination of married women

Table 7.4   Support for Expanding Ordination: Subgroups, 1999

	Ordain Married Men %	Return to Priesthood %	Ordain Married Women %	Ordain Celibate Women %
Gender				
Men	69	75	52	61
Women	72	79	55	63
Generation				
Post–Vatican II	71	81	60	71
Vatican II	72	77	55	62
Pre–Vatican II	66	72	40*	49*
Education				
High school or less	66	73	49*	59
Some college	72	79	56	61
College degree or more	78	82	57	68
Catholic Education				
1–6 years	70	75	54	62
7–12 years	72	79	51	59
13 or more years	55*	65*	43*	51*
Church Commitment				
High	57*	65*	31*	42*
Family Income				
Less than $30,000	66	73	49*	59
$30,000–$50,000	73	76	52	56
$50,000–$75,000	79	89	62	72
$75,000 or more	72	78	55	69

*The percentage is much lower than average in the column

(between 51 and 62 percent). Subgroups with less than 50 percent approval were those with the most Catholic schooling (43 percent), the highly committed (31 percent), the oldest generation (40 percent), those with incomes below $30,000 (49 percent), and those with education at the high-school level or below (49 percent).

Table 7.4 shows that a growing majority of Catholics in almost every category agreed that "it would be a good thing if" ordination were expanded to formerly active priests (men, 75 percent; women, 79 percent); to married men (men, 69 percent; women, 72 percent); to celibate women (men, 61 percent; women, 63 percent); and to married women (men, 52 percent; women, 55 percent). Not only did men and women agree, the differences between them were generally small.

Respondents from different generations also generally agreed, except over the issue of ordaining women. All generations supported reactivating former priests; post-Vatican II and Vatican II Catholics were somewhat more positive than older people (81 percent, 77 percent, and 72 percent, respectively). The same pattern held for ordaining married men (younger and middle cohorts, 71 percent and 72 percent; older cohort, 66 percent). Younger Catholics favored ordaining celibate women more than did older Catholics, with post-Vatican II Catholics being more positive (71 percent) than Vatican II or pre-Vatican II cohorts (62 percent and 49 percent). The younger and Vatican II generations (60 percent and 55 percent respectively) favored ordaining married women; the pre-Vatican II cohort did not (40 percent approved). In sum, both genders and the younger generations supported extending the priestly ministry to men and women, married or not. Older Catholics were less in favor of ordaining women.

One of the most influential subgroups throughout the study was high commitment Catholics identified by the Church Commitment Index. Sixty-five percent of Catholics who scored highest on the index thought formerly active priests should be reinstated, and 57 percent favored ordaining married men. Forty-two percent approved of ordaining celibate women, and an even smaller percentage (31 percent) approved of ordaining married women. On all four issues they were less in favor than other Catholics.

In general, there was support for expanding ordination from both men and women; all generations; and all levels of commitment, education, and income. However, the ordination of women, especially of married women, continues to meet with opposition from the pre-Vatican II cohort and the most committed Catholics.

Because Latino Catholics are the fastest growing segment of the U.S. Catholic population, we studied their views on ordaining women. As do the vast majority of Catholic subgroups, more than 60 percent of Latinos favored the ordination of celibate women and just under 60 percent, married women. In fact, they were slightly more approving than non-Latinos. Given the overall support of expanding ordination even in the swelling Latino population, we expect receptivity to ordination of not only married men but also women to grow in the future.

CONCLUSION

In this chapter we have discussed the findings of the report commissioned in 1998 by the U.S. National Conference of Catholic Bishops and traced the clergy decline that led to the current priest shortage. We have presented some options to increase the Church workforce, such as expanding women's roles and increasing ordination of male deacons. While the problem is being addressed, it is far from being solved.

In our surveys in 1987, 1993, and 1999, we asked the laity about its views on tackling the problem and adjusting to clergy shortages over time. We asked about scaling down services and found more overall endorsement for changes in parish management than for any reductions in pastoral services that priests typically perform. We also found an increasing acceptance over time for the ordination of married men and women.

The laity seemed aware of the problems of priest shortages and willing to tackle them in creative ways. As they focused on ways to maintain, build, and strengthen community (Wittberg 1996), the laity expressed ideas centered on doing things differently so that the ministry could be preserved and enlarged. Whatever the future holds, it is clear that the laity wants to retain strong parishes and priestly services and welcomes new administrative arrangements and expansion of priestly roles in order to do so.

Chapter Eight

Participation, Democracy, and Decision Making

Newman and Halvorson (2000, 70–72) have described the transformation of the Catholic Church since 1900:

> In little more than a century, what had been a small and marginalized, almost cell-like presence had been completely transformed. It is a testament to the genius and organizational strength of the Catholic Church that in a century characterized by the proliferation of religious organizations based on ethnic differences, regionalism, and theological disputes, the Catholic Church managed these potentially divisive forces within a single unitary organizational substructure. Though differences might exist between individual parishes or between dioceses, the overarching structure remained intact. By 1950 Catholic Church parishes were to be found in all states, and by 1990 all but 40 counties had at least one parish. [Now] at the beginning of the 21st century, the Catholic Church has been accepted as part of the mainstream of American religious life, and therefore, almost certainly is one of, if not the most national denomination.

In chapter 1 we pointed out how the combination of factors such as immigration, education, and occupational mobility made this transformation possible. Still, it was the hierarchical, bureaucratic governing structure preaching a doctrine of conformity to its teachings that brought it about. Our research has shown that the Catholic laity still has a high level of conformity to basic tenets of faith, such as the nature of the sacraments, the Resurrection, and the Real Presence of Christ in the Eucharist, while at the same time it has moved away from strict adherence to church rules regarding such things as Mass attendance and contraceptive birth control. Perhaps it may seem strange that Catholics, having achieved a high level of personal freedom in a large mainstream American religion, want more participation in church governance. It is because the adoption of Vatican II reforms and renewal of parish life, plus the priest shortage (documented in chapter 7), have dramatically altered the social context of parish life.[1] Catholic Church life has changed, and this has affected the feelings of laypeople.

In this chapter we review some of the factors that have led to the existing governing structure and decision-making processes of the Church, citing scholarly writings that support the legitimacy of the magisterium and others that argue for a more broad-based decision-making structure. We then discuss trends in replies to questions we have been asking about democratic decision making in the Church and some specific issues that have come to the fore in recent years. We conclude with a look at three new items added to the 1999 survey having to do with the laity's perception of how priests view them and the laity's evaluation of clergy and church leaders. Our findings show that the laity wants a more participative church and that a large amount of laity attention is directed to the local parish.

THE AMERICAN CATHOLIC EXPERIENCE

The desire of laity today for a more active role in church governance has roots in long-term American culture as well as in the stimulus of Vatican II documents. If you ask Americans whether they would like the right to participate in *any* kind of decision making—religious or not—they are likely to respond in the affirmative, because it is a deeply ingrained value in American culture.

From the time of the appointment of the first bishop in the United States, John Carroll, in 1789, through the late nineteenth century, an "Americanist" movement made itself heard in the United States. "It advocated moving the Church in the direction of American values: separation of church and state, cooperation with other Christian denominations, autonomy from the Vatican, religious liberty under the law, and more democratic decision making in the Church" (D'Antonio et al. 1996, 7ff). By the end of the nineteenth century, the

---

1. We have already cited the research of Murnion and DeLambo (1999), which shows that more than 30,000 laypeople work in a variety of administrative roles at the parish and diocesan levels in the United States. Wallace (1992) documents the growing role of women in running priestless parishes; she is currently writing a book on priestless parishes run by men. Yet Catholic laity have generally been outside the power loop in most decisions, such as those affecting parish life and whether to close parishes.

die was cast for suppression of this model with the issuance by Pope Leo XIII of his letter *Testem Benevolentiae* in which he chastised the Americanist effort and reaffirmed the traditional European model of Church governance. Dolan (1985, 224) sums up the situation:

> Catholicism was now deemed a religion of hierarchical authority, and people learned not only to pray, but also to obey. Being Catholic meant to submit to the authority of God as mediated through the Church—its Pope, bishops, and pastors. In such a culture, the rights of the individual conscience were deemphasized, as each person was conditioned to submit to the external authority of the Church.

In the first half of the twentieth century, American Catholics managed to adapt to the Vatican model while also growing increasingly comfortable with America's secular culture, with its emphasis on democracy and individual freedom. Then came Vatican II and its acceptance of important features of this secular culture, including freedom of conscience and religion. Afterward, in the latter part of the twentieth century, the Roman Catholic church moved back toward more centralized authority. How and why did these changes happen?

Scholars who have dug into the footnotes of history have uncovered enough evidence to raise doubts that a monarchical, centralized governing structure has been the only, or preferred, structure of the Church throughout two millenia (Bianchi and Ruether 1992; Quinn 1999). Bianchi and Ruether (1992, 12) offer two reasons why it is legitimate for the Catholic laity to speak out and to work for reform of the church structure.

First, today people understand that all social structures are human creations. The structures are, accordingly, historical and subject to revision. This view better explains the way that the current structure evolved in history than is the assertion that it was foreordained by God to be hierarchical and controlled by celibate men.[2] Second, we have slowly come to recognize that democratic, participatory forms of government are more appropriate for the respect of people and for safeguarding against abusive relationships than hierarchical and

---

2. Dulles disagrees and deemphasizes the historical changes in the Catholic Church. He acknowledges (1998, 10) that religious language is historically and culturally conditioned, but insists that "the truths expressed by it, inasmuch as they are warranted by God, transcend that conditioning." Further, he asserts that "historicism undermines the view of orthodox Christianity that the revelation given in Christ and the articles of Christian faith are permanently valid" (ibid., 12).

monarchical systems unmindful of human rights.[3] The debate today is about the extent to which some kind of decision-making model can be developed within the current bureaucratic organization, so the laity will have some voice. Many influential leaders are apprehensive. For his part, Dulles (1998, 13) expresses the fears of many in the church magisterium that "the attempt to apply democratic principles to the Church threatens the Church's claim to possession of certain truths, and more dangerous still, would require that church leaders would have to adjust their teachings in light of public opinion polls or democratic votes." Others disagree. Archbishop John Quinn (1999) acknowledges the concerns that have led Pope John Paul II to revert to more centralized control of the Church, yet he advocates development of the doctrine of collegiality outlined at Vatican II and insists that this doctrine is essential to the Church's efforts to preach the Gospel of Christ effectively.

Are the fears of Dulles and members of the hierarchy warranted? Are these fears blocking new leadership that could revitalize the Church? What do the laity mean when they say they want the right to participate in church governance?

Vatican II and Beyond: Varieties of Decision-Making Models

Archbishop John Quinn states, based on his own readings in church history: "Neither Catholic doctrine nor divine tradition indicates that the Pope should fulfill his mission by an elaborate centralization such as we have today" (1999, 115). The laity we surveyed agree. They find theological support in the Vatican II documents for more active lay participation. They point to the Council

---

3. Among the central points raised by the contributors to the Bianchi–Ruether volume (1992) on democracy in the Catholic Church, a few are relevant here: (1) Fiorenza acknowledges that it is not possible to prove that the early Christians organized themselves into a democratic community any more than it can be proved that the early Church was a pure patriarchy. (2) Bianchi traces the growth of anti-democratic structures in the Church in the late nineteenth and early twentieth centuries to the *Syllabus of Errors* of Pius IX and to Vatican I with its emphasis on papal power and infallibility. (3) Beal examines the canonical heritage and concludes that Vatican II brought the Church back to where it was in the medieval era: "face to face with the communion of the people of God, hierarchically ordered but endowed with a fundamental equality," which can eventually lead to a more democratic church (p. 75). (4) In his historical review, Curran concludes that the Church has always reflected societal structures in its own structures; thus there is no divine model handed down from on high, but only human models. Curran then raises the question, "What human model best serves the people of God in its present circumstances?" (p. 95).

itself as one of the great exemplary collegial experiences of the twentieth century: more than two thousand bishops met in vibrant dialogue over a period of three years and brought forth important structural, liturgical, and doctrinal changes. The changes had the support of the great majority of the bishops and the rest of the worldwide Church. The council documents provided a new collegial model for church governance. They spoke of a more collegial church, of a more active role for the laity, and of a more decentralized governing structure. They re-visioned the Church as the People of God.

The bishops adopted these documents by a formal vote after lengthy discussion and intense debate. To the extent that the bishops could be said to be representing the people of their dioceses, the decision making during Vatican II constituted a democratic process. Church leaders preferred to call this a "collegial," not a democratic process, but many laypeople saw it as a step in the direction of a more democratic Church.

Another notable act of leadership and broad participation was the creation by Pope John XXIII of the Papal Birth Control Commission in the 1960s.[4] The commission, which began in 1963 with six members, gradually expanded to fifty-five members. For the final and decisive session, seven cardinals and five other bishops were added (two bishops had been appointed earlier). The commission included eleven theologians, seven sociologists, five gynecologists, five demographers, three economists, representatives of other church organizations, representatives of civil and government agencies, and several laypeople. The members had a broad range of racial, national, and ethnic backgrounds, and had deep concerns about the Church's teachings on birth control. They pondered why the teachings could or could not be changed (McClory 1995).

Although the commission met in secrecy for several years, its deliberations gradually became known. Later they were published, including the final report to the pope. We now know that only four of the fifty-five members rejected the final report, which concluded that it was possible for the Church to change its teachings on birth control even while maintaining a central place in marriage for conjugal love and responsible parenthood. The great majority of cardinals and bishops voted to approve the majority report; one cardinal was openly opposed to change; and another remained silent.

A reading of the commission documents reveals a wide range of belief about the Church's teaching on birth control, from the position that the teaching was

---

4. For an insider's account of the deliberations of the Papal Birth Control Mission, see Robert McClory, *Turning Point* (1995), giving accounts by some of the lay members, especially Patty Crowley, cofounder of the Christian Family Movement. See also Robert Blair Kaiser, *The Politics of Sex and Religion* (1985), a detailed description of the commission's work and setting.

constant and inerrant to the belief that new understandings in biology, sexuality, and marriage would make possible changes in the teachings. Pope Paul VI rejected the commission's recommendation for a change in the teaching on birth control and reaffirmed the traditional teaching. He acknowledged the majority report of the commission but dismissed it as not definitive. Instead, he relied heavily on a special report given to him by the minority of four, written without consultation with other members of the commission.

The majority of Catholics in the United States and elsewhere in the Western world, many of whom had closely followed the Papal Birth Control Commission's debates, had expected change and thus rejected Pope Paul VI's reaffirmation of the traditional teaching. In deciding against the great majority, the pope not only undercut the three-year effort of the commission but also brought into question the relevance and validity of Chapter 12 of *Lumen Gentium* (Light of the Nations), an important document of Vatican II. This chapter says, "The body of the faithful as a whole, anointed as they are by the Holy One" (cf. Jn. 2:20, 27), cannot err in matters of belief. Thanks to a supernatural sense of the faith which characterizes the People as a whole, it manifests this unerring quality, when, from the bishops down to the last member of the laity, it shows universal agreement in matters of faith and morals" (Abbott 1966, 29).

It has often been said that for any teaching to be effective it must be not only proclaimed by the Vatican but also accepted by the whole body of the Church. In this sense, the Church is the whole people of God, including the laity, the clergy, the bishops, and the pope. Clearly, the whole Church is not united on the issue of birth control. The gap between the Vatican's position and the laity's attitude today is a sign that *Humanae Vitae* is far from being accepted as an eternal truth.

Experiments in Collegiality in the U.S. Church

Three important events in the 1980s and 1990s demonstrated that the Church in the United States can act effectively in a collegial manner. We commented on two of them in chapter 6: the issuance of the U.S. bishops' pastoral letter on peace and their letter on economic justice for all. The letters were published only after much input from the laity from all points on the ideological spectrum. The process was collegial among the bishops and also collegial among all Catholics in that it included important contributions from laity—conservatives, liberals, and moderates—which greatly influenced the final text. The third event of importance was the issuance of the letter on the place of women in the Church. Written in the early 1990s, it was steadfastly opposed by many women's groups from a wide range of positions. In the end, it failed to gain the necessary two-thirds vote of the bishops to make it an official pastoral letter, and the matter was dropped. The failure to gain the necessary votes has been deemed a victory for the voice of the laity, in this case the women, whose objections convinced the bishops that lay acceptance would be impossible. What these examples–Vatican II and the U.S. bishops' pastorals–have in common is that they produced documents after long and extensive debate, argument, revisions, and further revisions. Most important, a majority of Catholics familiar with these documents supported them.

Not all Catholics today desire change. Many Catholics who want a Church with more lay participation in decision making are nevertheless sympathetic to a very slow rate of change. For example, here is a statement by a church member active in social justice issues:

> The Catholic Church is very slow to change. You have to appreciate that. I respect that, even when I know it is making mistakes. But now we have Vatican II reforms, and that is enough; it calls us to live the Gospel. We cannot wait for more reforms of the Church. We have to go out and live the Gospel.

Other Catholics have grown tired of the Church's current governing structure. Here is a statement by a former Catholic:[5] "Why did I leave the Catholic Church? Because the Church's power structure is outdated." In Lee and D'Antonio's (2000) nationwide survey, 17 percent of the sample said they had been born and raised Catholic but had left the Church and no longer considered themselves Catholic. Half of them said that their main reason for leaving the Church was that its power structure was outdated.

Lay Attitudes toward Participation in Church Decision Making

Our 1999 data show that the laity believe they have a right to participate in church decision making, a belief shared by men and women and by all three generations. Even the most highly committed Catholics want more participation. The feeling is widespread. In chapter 1 we sketched out the process by which the Catholic Church in the United States became transformed at the social, institutional, and personal levels. Chapter 4 showed a lessening of obedience to church teachings in such matters as marriage, Mass attendance, and reception of the sacraments. Chapter 5 made clear that a growing number of laypeople believe that final moral authority should rest with them as individ-

---

5. Both statements are from telephone interviews of a 1996 national sample of Catholics. See Lee and D'Antonio, 2000, Appendix II, 186.

uals as they make decisions thoughtfully and take responsibility for their own behavior. In chapter 7 we found a gap between the thinking of the laity and the hierarchy on the priest shortage and the role of women in the Church. The data in these chapters show that laypeople are more and more making decisions for themselves that are at variance with church teachings. We now ask, more specifically, what is their attitude toward more democratic decision making in the Catholic Church? Given the freedoms they have, what more do they want?

Table 8.1 shows the trends in replies to the question "Some people think that the Catholic Church should have more democratic decision making in church affairs that do not involve matters of faith than it has at the present time. Do you favor or oppose this idea?"

Already in 1987 a majority of Catholics favored more democratic decision making at all levels of the Church. They made a modest distinction between the local parish level and the more distant Vatican level, and that distinction has remained constant over time. Support for more democratic decision making grew gradually from 1987 to 1999. We looked to see if men and women agreed, if the generations agreed, and if the persons high or low in church commitment agreed (see table 8.2), and we found similar trends in all the subgroups. In each survey we found small differences between men and women, with the men slightly more supportive of democratic decision making than the women. The generations differed in their views: in 1987, pre–Vatican II Catholics were the least likely to support more democratic decision making at any of the three church levels, but later these oldest Catholics changed more than other Catholics, so that by 1999 they were little different from younger persons. Having strong commitment to the Church did not seem to have much effect on these attitudes; in all three surveys the highly committed gave as much support to more democratic decision making as the less committed.

To measure Catholic attitudes toward particular areas of decision making, we asked: "For each of the following areas of church life, please tell me if you think the Catholic laity should have the right to participate, or should not have the right to participate?" (see table 8.3). We asked specifically whether the laity should have the right to participate in deciding how parish income should be spent, in

Table 8.1.   Catholic Laity Who Favor More Democratic Decision Making in Church Affairs

	1987 %	1993 %	1999 %
At the parish level	60	61	66
At the diocesan level	55	60	61
At the Vatican level	51	58	55

Table 8.2. Support for More Democratic Decision Making, by Three Generations and by High-Commitment Catholics

	1987 Generations			1999 Generations		
	Pre–Vatican II %	Vatican II %	Post–Vatican II %	Pre–Vatican II %	Vatican II %	Post-Vatican II %
At parish level	49	66	64	66	69	65
At diocesan level	46	64	53	59	68	55
At Vatican level	43	58	51	52	60	52

	1987 High-Commitment Catholics %	1999 High-Commitment Catholics %
At parish level	64	65
At diocesan level	61	56
At Vatican level	55	51

selecting parish priests, and in deciding whether women should be ordained to the priesthood. These topics are diverse, and the attitudes turned out to be diverse.

In all three surveys the vast majority believed that laity should have the right to participate in how parish income is spent (80 percent or more agreed).[6] On helping to select parish priests, there was an increase in support between 1987 and 1999. A similar pattern occurred on whether laity should participate in the decision about ordaining women. The percentage saying yes jumped from 48 percent in 1987 to 63 percent in 1999. The attitudes of men and women were similar on spending parish income and selecting priests, but on the issue of deciding about women's ordination, women's support increased from 1987 to 1999 more than did men's.

We found little variation among the three generations on the issues of lay participation in spending parish income: all strongly agreed. On the issue of selecting priests, the pre–Vatican II Catholics were less in favor than the others. Similarly, on the issue of women's ordination, that cohort was less in favor of lay involvement.

---

6. Zaleski and Zech (1994) had found that members of parishes with more active participation by laity in parish decision making, especially regarding the use of parish funds, were more likely to make larger financial contributions to the parish. However, the Hoge et al. study (1996) tested the same hypothesis and found little support for it. Rather, Hoge and his associates found that dissatisfaction with the decision-making process, whatever the process is, predicts lower giving. If the laity is satisfied, the nature of the parish decision-making process does not seem to matter.

Table 8.3.   Support for Catholic Laity's Right to Participate in Decision Making

	1987 (%)	1999 (%)
Deciding Local Parish Issues		
How parish income is spent	81	82
Selecting priests for parish	57	73
Deciding an Institutional Issue		
Deciding about ordaining women	48	63

	Generations in 1987			Generations in 1999		
	Pre–Vatican II %	Vatican II %	Post–Vatican II %	Pre–Vatican II %	Vatican II %	Post–Vatican II %
How parish income is spent	76	85	81	75	84	84
Selecting priests	50	57	69	58	69	81
Ordaining women	34	55	57	44	62	71

	1987 High-Commitment Catholics %	1999 High-Commitment Catholics %
How parish income is spent	86	80
Selecting priests	46	59
Ordaining women	40	45

High-commitment Catholics were as supportive as others regarding lay involvement in deciding how parish funds are spent. Regarding selecting priests for parishes, they moved over time from having a minority (46 percent in 1987) in support of the idea to having a majority (59 percent in 1999). Even on the question of women's ordination, their support increased from 40 percent to 45 percent. This is cause for reflection. In the late 1990s, although Rome declared the question of women's ordination closed, it appears that many even of the most highly committed Catholics continue to think they have a right to talk about it.

The trend is clear: Catholics feel more and more strongly about the right to have democratic decision making and lay participation in the Church. Only among the pre–Vatican II generation and those most highly committed to the Church was there less than majority support, and then only on the issue of deciding about women's ordination.

New Trends: A Case in Point

The increasing participation of the laity at the parish and diocesan levels, well documented in recent research by Murnion and DeLambo (1999), is not without its ups and downs. Tussles over centralized control versus local control are inevitable. A newspaper story (Barnhart 2000) illustrates the problems. A woman who had served as director of the Catholic Campus Ministry program at Western Washington University for fifteen years was replaced by a priest. Church officials explained they had discussed the matter with her, and that it was simply standard policy. Meanwhile, students and faculty were outraged at the action, which was taken without any consultation with them. One of the parish trustees, a retired professor, acknowledged that "I'm not saying it is unreasonable to have a priest or that the archdiocese doesn't have the authority to do that. However, they are digging into a successful program that is very popular with students." A senior undergraduate declared: "She brings real social justice to the program here. For a lot of students here, that's what keeps them in the church. . . . She's very welcoming to gay and lesbian Catholics and very supportive of women."

Archdiocesan leaders insisted that the action was merely a restructuring and that the director was in good standing with the diocese. Another professor who had worked closely with the center said, "This is a time when we should be fostering more female leadership within the Church, and it does bother me. What kind of message does this send especially to young women who aspire for leadership positions within the Church?"

Mixed Feelings about Parishes and Priests

Our final table provides insights about the climate for structural changes. Table 8.4 shows that by an overwhelming 91 percent, the laity thinks parish priests do a good job. A small majority (53 percent) think church leaders are out of touch with the laity. A large minority (46 percent) think today's parishes are too big and impersonal, and a similar minority (44 percent) think that priests see lay people only as followers, not leaders. The attitudes are mixed.

We found few differences between men and women on these issues. When we compared generations, only one distinctive difference appeared: Pre–Vatican II Catholics were less likely than the post–Vatican II Catholics (38 percent and 50 percent) to agree with the statement that parishes had grown too big and impersonal. When we compared high-commitment and low-commitment Catholics, we found significant differences. The former were the least likely (31 percent) to say that priests don't expect the laypeople to be leaders, just followers; they were also the least likely to say that parishes had grown too big and impersonal (30 percent) and least likely to say that church leaders were out of touch with the laity (38 percent). Catholics of all levels of commitment agreed on one thing: parish priests do a good job. These findings are important. Catholics who are the most committed to the Church saw the local

Table 8.4. Attitudes about Priests, Church Leaders, and Parishes, 1999 (percentage agreeing with each statement)

	Generations				*Level of Commitment*		
		Pre–Vatican II	*Vatican II*	*Post–Vatican II*			
	Total	*II*	*II*	*II*	*High*	*Medium*	*Low*
	%	*%*	*%*	*%*	*%*	*%*	*%*
On the whole, parish priests do a good job.	91	92	87	90	95	92	83
Catholic church leaders are out of touch with the laity.	53	48	56	51	38	60	67
Catholic parishes are too big and impersonal.	46	38	45	50	30	49	62
Most priests don't expect the lay members to be leaders, just followers.	44	43	42	48	31	50	54

parish in a much more favorable light than did less committed Catholics. Were church leaders to move toward more collegial governing structures, the laity participating most would probably be these highly committed persons.

CONCLUSIONS

The foregoing look at history helps us understand American Catholics' desire for a more active role in church governance. The Catholic Church in the United States began with a strong Americanist tone, but over the course of the nineteenth century it came more and more under centralized Vatican control, the high point being Vatican Council I in 1870, when the bishops declared the pope to be infallible under certain conditions. In the mid-twentieth century the prevailing vision shifted, resulting in the more participative documents of Vatican II in 1962–1965, which called for a more collegial relationship between the pope and the bishops. The documents supported political democracies, and they supported freedom of conscience and religious belief in all nations. More than that, people who lived during Vatican II witnessed a church in full debate over its nature, its norms, and its raison d'être. The desire by today's laity for a more open, democratic Church builds on the experience of Vatican II, the peace and economy pastorals in the 1980s, and the general ethos of American society.

Organizations that follow democratic principles recognize the legitimacy of a pluralism of views and the right of members to strive to make their voices heard in peaceful discussion, debate, and voting. Members have the right to change laws and rules when they make decisions using clearly spelled-out procedures. The Catholic Church has never been, nor is it likely to become, a democratic organization in that sense. The desires of participation-minded laypeople are more limited. Most of them, as far as we can determine, want the right to participate in the discussions and debates central to decision making, and they can point to events like Vatican Council II and the U.S. Bishops' pastoral letters as models of collaboration. Today some collaboration of this kind seems to exist, mainly at the local parish level and mainly with regard to practical matters such as finances.

The laity is not alone in the quest for a more collegial church. Bishops and theologians are also debating the issues. This is exemplified by Archbishop John Quinn's book, *Reform of the Papacy* (1999). The book is a reasoned argument for church reforms to give more influence to local bishops vis-a-vis the Curia in Rome, and more influence to laypeople in collaboration with the bishops in local dioceses. Although Quinn does not speak directly to the issues raised in this or preceding chapters, he makes proposals for reform that would lead to more active lay participation in decision making at all levels of church life. He offers these recommendation for reform: (a) fewer bishops and more laypeople in the Curia and other administrative offices; (b) limited terms for Curia heads; (c) more support for the principles of subsidiarity, collegiality, and decentralization; and (d) appointment of a special papal commission for recommending curial reforms, to consist of a bishop as president, a representative of the Curia, and a layperson (1999: 172–77). Quinn fears that leaving the system unchanged will lead to obsolescence and fragmentation. He worries that failure to implement the principles of subsidiarity and collegiality will result in great disorder later, because the Church will not be able to respond to the rapid changes in the world. The American Catholic laity seem ready to join in this renewal effort.

Chapter Nine

Summary and Implications

The first part of this chapter serves as an executive summary of our research. Then we address the implications our findings have for the Catholic Church.

WHAT WE HAVE LEARNED

In chapter 1, we described important changes in the status of Catholics in the United States. We also identified continuities and changes in the norms and values of the Church itself. Our review of these developments led to a number of questions about trends and variations in Catholics' beliefs and practices. In chapter 2, we examined numerous influences to see which were most strongly associated with Catholics' views of faith and morals. Three stood out: gender, generation, and commitment to the Church. As a result, these three influences are the foci of our analysis. Other factors, such as race, parishioner status, Catholic schooling, and income exert selected influences that we summarize in appendix A and appendix B.

Major Findings

We divide our major findings into two parts: trends and the effects of gender, generation, and commitment to the Church.

Trends.

In chapter 3, we showed that most Catholics still think of themselves as Catholic and cannot imagine belonging to some other religious tradition. Their Catholic identity includes firm belief in a number of teachings grounded in the Nicene Creed and two millennia of Catholic tradition. Although Catholics clearly embrace the idea of being Catholic, follow many core Church teachings, and feel some obligation to support their local parishes, their attachment to the institutional Church is slipping. In chapter 4, we reported that weekly Mass attendance and reception of Holy Communion have declined since the 1950s. Though Catholics are not receiving Communion as often as earlier, or as often as Church leaders would like, a majority still believes in the Real Presence and reports that this belief is a very important component of its personal faith. Private confession with a priest also is far less common than it used to be. Though Catholics report that they pray frequently, there is a decline in traditional devotional practices, and less than one-quarter of Catholics participate in Scripture-oriented practices such as reading the Bible and Bible study groups. There is a trend to interfaith marriage, and Catholics are increasingly marrying outside the Church.

Chapter 5 showed that American Catholics are less inclined to grant Church leaders "final say" on sexual and reproductive matters such as divorce and remarriage, contraception, abortion, sexual relations outside marriage, and homosexual activity. Increasingly, they feel that laypeople have responsibility for their own decisions in such matters, or that Church leaders and laypeople should collaborate in formulating Church norms in these areas. Chapter 6 indicated that half or more of Catholics agree with Church leaders on increased spending on health care for poor children, reduced spending on the military, and reductions in nuclear weapons. A majority also agrees that welfare cutbacks have gone far enough. However, contrary to Church teachings, a majority believes in stricter enforcement of the death penalty, and an increasing percentage of Catholics (now slightly more than half) believe one can be a good Catholic without donating time or money to help the poor.

Chapter 7 indicated that Catholics continue to believe in the importance of the sacraments and want them to be available on a regular basis. At the same time, Catholics are more and more comfortable with parishes being administered by laypeople and visiting priests. Though they do not see communion services as acceptable alternatives to Masses led by priests, they are increasingly willing to accept them as occasional substitutes. Wanting to protect the sacraments as much as possible, a growing majority of Catholics, including a majority of those who are highly committed to the Church, are willing to expand the concept of priesthood to include women and, especially, married men. Chapter 8 showed that the percentage of Catholics wanting more democratic decision making in the Church grew between 1987 and 1999.

Variations.

Commitment to the Church correlates with most of the beliefs and practices we have examined. Overall, Catholics who are most highly attached to the Church also are most inclined to look to Church leaders as authorities in the areas of faith and morals, and they are most likely to agree with official Church teachings. They also are most likely to participate in the sacraments and a whole range of devotional practices. Catholics at all levels of commitment are increasingly willing to ordain women and married men, although highly committed Catholics are most reluctant to do so. Commitment to the Church has no discernible impact on the way Catholics viewed cutbacks in sacramental services. It also has no appreciable effect on Catholics' preferences for more democratic decision making in the Church. Nor does it affect their assessment of parish priests and church leaders.

Generation also has significant effects. The biggest generational differences are between the pre–Vatican II and Vatican II generations, but there also are sizable differences between the Vatican II and post–Vatican II generations. These differences indicate a continuing shift from higher to lower levels of community and from compliance with traditional teachings to greater autonomy. We find no evidence that the youngest generation is returning to the views of the pre–Vatican II generation.

Gender also has important effects. Women are more religiously active than men, but are now less willing than men are to grant Church leaders final say on matters of sexual and reproductive ethics. Women also are more inclined to say that one cannot be a good Catholic without donating time and money to help the poor. They also are more likely to support spending on health care for poor children, less likely to favor the death penalty, and less likely to spend money on the military. Women are not as accepting of a reduction in sacramental services as men are. Catholic men and women are more similar than different in the extent and nature of their Catholic identity; their tendency to marry other Catholics and to marry in the Church; and their views on the ordination of men and women and decision making in the Church.

Through a separate series of statistical analyses (known as path analyses), we are able to illustrate the way gender, generation, and commitment affect Catholics' beliefs and practices. Let us explain, starting from the left side of figure 9.1. First, there is a small, but statistically significant, relationship between gender and generation. This relationship indicates that there are more women than men in the pre–Vatican II generation. Second, generation affects commitment to the Church. Pre–Vatican II Catholics are more highly committed to the Church than Vatican II and post–Vatican II Catholics. Third, gender also affects commitment, with women being more attached to the Church than men. Thus, some of the effect that gender and generation have on Catholics' beliefs and practices is indirect, through their impact on commitment.

Fourth, controlling for these indirect effects, we find that gender and generation have direct effects of their own. In other words, men and women with similar levels of commitment to the Church still have somewhat different beliefs

Figure 9.1.   The Effects of Gender, Generation, and Commitment to the Church on Religious Beliefs and Practices

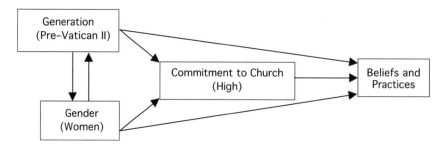

and practices. Likewise, pre–Vatican II, Vatican II, and post–Vatican II Catholics with similar levels of commitment are still different from one another in some respects. Overall, being a woman and belonging to the pre–Vatican II generation increases the likelihood that one will have rather traditional beliefs and practices, whereas being male and belonging to the post–Vatican II generation increases the likelihood that one will tend to disagree with church teachings. Finally, commitment to the Church has the strongest, most direct, and most consistent effect on the beliefs and practices we have studied. The more committed a Catholic is to the Church, the more likely he or she is to embrace Church teachings. The less committed one is to the Church, the more one is inclined toward beliefs and practices that do not conform to Church norms.

The magnitude of these effects varies somewhat according to the belief or practice being considered. For example, commitment has a strong impact on Catholics' tendency to say that one cannot be a good Catholic without going to Mass, that they pray regularly, and that they oppose the ordination of married men and married women. It has relatively little impact on their views of democratic decision making in the Church (indicating that Catholics at all levels of commitment prefer this arrangement). Generation has a strong effect on the frequency of prayer and the preference for lay participation in decisions about selecting parish priests and the ordination of men and women. It, like commitment, is of very little consequence when it comes to democratic decision making in the Church. Gender's strongest effects are in the frequency of private prayer and decisions about the ordination of women. Gender doesn't have much bearing on one's identification as a Catholic or one's interest in democratic decision making.

These findings confirm the results of other research showing considerable agreement among Catholics on core teachings related to the Trinity, Incarnation, Resurrection, Mary as the Mother of God, Christ's presence in the sacraments, and concern for the poor. Our data also confirm previous research documenting declines in religious practice and a shift from tradition to conscience.

They reconfirm studies pointing to generation as an important source of pluralism in today's Church and indicate, once again, the role that commitment to the Church plays in shaping Catholics' views of faith and morals. Although Catholic men and women have similar views of many issues, our data are consistent with other work showing that there are some discernible differences in the way men and women look at faith and morals. Our findings also are consistent with other studies showing that interfaith marriage is increasing.

IMPLICATIONS FOR THE CHURCH

Our findings contribute to an understanding of community and autonomy in today's Church. They also have implications for ministering to Catholics who differ in gender, generation, and levels of commitment to the Church.

Trends in Community and Autonomy

In chapter 2, we introduced a figure with a vertical axis depicting high to low levels of participation in a Catholic community and a horizontal axis ranging from conformity to external authority to autonomy based on internal authority. If Church history teaches us anything, it is that the Church's location along these axes constantly changes. There are periods of intense community life, and periods when participation is low. There are times when conformity transcends autonomy, and times when autonomy prevails over conformity.

In the pre–Vatican II years of, let us say, the 1950s, American Catholics were highly involved in their Catholic communities, and they tended to comply with Church doctrines. Research by Lenski (1961) and others showed that the pre–Vatican II years produced very high levels of religious practice and quite extraordinary levels of agreement on a wide range of Church teachings. Mass attendance and reception of Holy Communion were frequent, and Catholics believed their church was the "one true Church." Catholics married other Catholics in the Church, and they tended to agree with the Church's teachings about sex and reproduction.

During this period, some Catholics were not religiously active and some found room to develop their own orientations to faith and morals without being excommunicated. Fichter's (1951) research showed that there were dormant and dissident Catholics back in the 1950s, but they were the exceptions to the rule. The pre–Vatican II years saw some inactivity in the midst of strong community life, and some autonomy in the midst of conformity.

Our data suggest that Catholics have moved toward lower levels of involvement in the community and increased levels of autonomy in the areas of faith and morals. Catholics are much more likely today than in the 1940s and '50s to formulate views of faith and morals that are based on their personal experiences and do not conform to Church teachings. Yet, it would be incorrect to say that American Catholics are completely individualistic and have abandoned all accountability to the Church. Despite the popularity of the all-too-glib phrase "cafeteria Catholic," American Catholics are not simply going down the line, picking and choosing whatever teachings satisfy their immediate appetites. They are in substantial agreement with Church teachings in many areas that are at the very heart of the Catholic tradition. There are important areas of unity in the midst of diversity.

Today's Catholics still think of themselves as Catholic and define a good Catholic as someone who accepts these core beliefs and lives according to them in their daily lives. Of the specifically religious practices we've examined, Catholics are still most likely to pray privately and participate in the sacraments. They respect the priesthood and think well of the priests in their parishes. Most still belong to a Catholic parish and the differences we found between parishioners and nonparishioners (see Appendix B) indicate that the parish still has an impact on the majority of Catholics who stay connected to one.

Yet, with their higher levels of education and worldly success, American Catholics are not as actively involved in the Catholic community as they once were, and they are more inclined to think and act autonomously. Catholics are no longer confined to the so-called Catholic ghetto. They are now free to participate in many aspects of civic life, and they do. As a result, the Church is no longer the focal point of their lives. It now is one among many commitments they make. They also are not as willing as they once were to subordinate themselves to Church authority. They are very American in their preference for democracy over more authoritarian forms of decision making. More than ever before, they are deciding how often they will attend Mass, whether to marry a Catholic, and what to believe about issues such as the ordination of women or the death penalty. They are no longer content to "pray, pay, and obey"; they prefer to "observe, judge, and act."

As figure 9.2 suggests, there are still significant levels of community life, but they are not as high as they were fifty years ago. Although community participation rates have declined, they have not hit bottom. There continue to be some areas of conformity, but Catholics are increasingly making up their own minds on many issues of faith and morals.

Community.

How much has the Catholic community declined? The answer depends on the criteria one uses to judge. Using the salience of Catholic identity as a criterion,

Figure 9.2. Recent Trends in American Catholicism

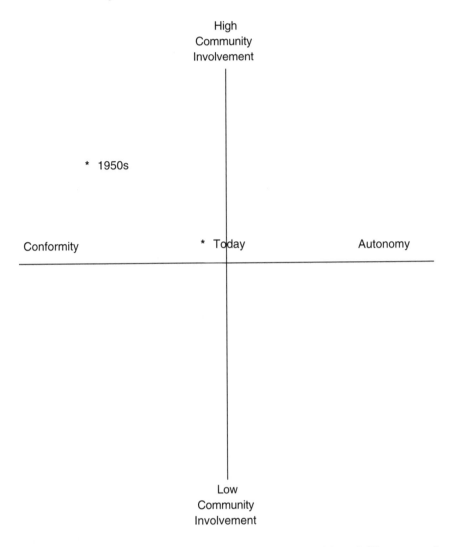

we estimate that community is down 20 to 30 percent. Although 72 percent of pre–Vatican II Catholics say there is something special about Catholicism that one cannot find in other faiths, only 54 percent of post–Vatican II believe that. Though 71 percent of pre–Vatican II Catholics say they cannot imagine being anything but Catholic, only 59 percent of post–Vatican II Catholics say that. Sixty–five percent of pre–Vatican II Catholics, but only 46 percent of the post–Vatican II generation say the Catholic Church is the "one true Church."

Only 28 percent of the pre–Vatican II generation says it could be just as happy in some other faith; 45 percent of the post–Vatican II generation says it could.

Using religious practice as a criterion, one could say with fairness that participation in Catholic community life is off about 35 to 45 percent. Frequency of private confession is down from 79 percent going at least once a year in the 1950s to only 43 percent going that often nowadays. Mass attendance is down from 75 percent attending weekly in the 1950s to only about 37 percent attending that often today. Getting married to another Catholic is down from 76 percent among pre–Vatican II Catholics to 60 percent among post–Vatican II Catholics. While 94 percent of pre–Vatican II Catholics who married a Catholic were married in the Church, that is true for only 71 percent of post–Vatican II Catholics who marry Catholics.

The trend lines in our data indicate that this loss of community will continue in the years ahead. All other things being equal, it is reasonable to predict that Catholics will be less attached to and involved in the Church twenty years from now. Levels of identification with and participation in the Church will continue to decline as the pre–Vatican II generation dies and the post–Vatican II generation (already nearly half of all Catholics eighteen years of age and older) becomes an even larger percentage of the Catholic population. We find very few, if any, indications of a reversal in the trend toward lower levels of community life.

The loss of community and the fear that it will continue are felt most acutely by pre–Vatican II Catholics who recall the "golden era" of the 1950s and compare it with today. However, the Catholic ghetto that produced extraordinarily high levels of communal involvement has nearly disappeared, so it is unrealistic to think that previously high levels of involvement could be achieved again. The sociological circumstances of today's American Catholics simply will not permit the high levels of community and conformity that were possible in the pre–Vatican II years of the 1940s and '50s. Young Catholics, by and large, do not sense much loss of community, because they have very little to compare with today's circumstances. They also do not seem as concerned about the prospects of further declines in community life. However, they need to appreciate that there is not as much Catholic community life today as there used to be, and that current trends toward lower levels of religious practice make older Catholics anxious about the future viability of the Church. They also need to realize that continuing declines in community life could jeopardize their access to the sacraments and sever their children's connection to the Church.

How can we increase involvement in the Catholic community? How can we increase Catholics' affective, or psychological, ties to the Church and their behavioral participation in its social and sacramental life? Research suggests three possibilities. Our first recommendation is to make sure the Church is meaningful to its members. If community is to develop, Catholics must have a sense that being Catholic is special. They must know how being Catholic is different from belonging to any other religious group. They must have pride in their heritage. Catholics can take pride in their tradition of sacramentalism and their extraordinary intellectual heritage. They should know about Catholic scholars such as Saint Thomas Aquinas, Rene Decartes, Cardinal John Newman, Teilhard de Chardin, and John Courtney Murray (to name just a few). They should appreciate that the Church has commissioned some of the world's greatest works of art, including the painting of the Last Supper and the ceiling of the Sistine Chapel. It also has produced some of the world's greatest artists (William Shakespeare, Leonardo DaVinci, Michelangelo, and Ludwig van Beethoven). It has a long history of saints, martyrs, and other models of holiness, such as Saint Francis of Assisi, Saint Elizabeth Seton, Archbishop Romero, Thomas Merton, and Dorothy Day. Its heritage includes a magnificent array of schools, hospitals, and orphanages. Catholic history includes a rich tradition of religious orders such as the Benedictines, the Franciscans, the Jesuits, and the Sisters of Charity. It also has a long-standing concern for the poor, exemplified in modern times by Mother Teresa, Cesar Chavez, and the Catholic Campaign for Human Development. Young Catholics need to learn about these wondrous historical achievements.

Of course, some parts of Catholic history are not so glorious. Although one need not agree with every one of his interpretations, Garry Wills (2000) makes a credible case that the Church has made poor judgments, acted unwisely, and been marred by scandal. It also is fair to say that the Vatican's recent decisions not to discuss the ordination of women, to limit divorced and remarried Catholics' access to the Eucharist, to terminate Sister Jeannine Gramick and Father Robert Nugent's ministry with gays and lesbians, and to resurrect barriers between Christian faiths have been troublesome for many faithful Catholics. Such events increase cynicism and alienation among many Catholics, especially today's young people, who are quick to dissociate themselves from hypocrisy. They make it difficult for a good many Catholics to take pride in their Church. For any attempt to build pride to be credible, it must acknowledge past failures. The pope's recent public apologies for past Catholic misdeeds are positive examples of such integrity. They demonstrate to all that the Church comprises human beings who sometimes fail, but as the Church asks us all to do, it acknowledges its sins and seeks to mend its ways. Any attempt to build pride also should minimize actions that pit claims of traditional authority against the laity's emphasis on reason. Given the laity's desire for a more collaborative form of decision making, the Church also should limit unilateral decisions on issues where it is known that Catholics of good faith hold differing views.

But enhancing group pride is not enough. There also is a need to strengthen relationships within and between groups of Catholics. This recommendation calls for building relationships within groups that have at least some attributes in common, such as young adults, Latinos/Latinas, retired men, homemakers, parents, new parishioners, senior citizens, schoolteachers, and business leaders. It also calls for the creation of ties across group lines. Here the goal is to bring together groups that might benefit from knowing one another better. Consider, for example, programs that bring parents of school-age children together with schoolteachers; college professors with high school students; and single men with single women. These relationships might be ends in themselves (satisfying Catholics' need for belonging), but they also might serve as means to other ends (locating people who can help one another); both are valuable.

Third, the Church must discern and try to meet the needs of its members. Some Catholics visit parishes, shopping for one that will meet their needs. These shoppers calculate the costs and benefits of belonging to different parishes, then select the one that promises the most rewards. Religious groups, both Catholic and non-Catholic, that are growing the most and are most successful in promoting a sense of community among members are especially good at identifying their members' social and spiritual needs, then meeting them. In the 1990s, many evangelical churches grew for just this reason. Willow Creek, a very successful Protestant congregation in the Chicago suburbs, has a famous knack for this. It has ministries for young executive women; women who have recently had abortions; single people under the age of 36, singles between 36 and 46, and singles over 46; men who want to discuss stock portfolios; and many others. It is not surprising that the members whose social needs are addressed during the week also pack the worship services on Sunday mornings. In our view, evangelical churches have a better record of discerning people's needs than Catholic parishes have. However, many Catholic parishes do an excellent job. For example, Holy Family Parish, not far from Willow Creek, has a similar ability to identify and meet the needs of its members. It does so with a staff that includes one priest and (at last count) thirty-six laypeople. It has a very strong sense of community in its parish life. Old St. Patrick's in Chicago is another parish that has gained a well-deserved reputation for discerning and meeting the needs of young adult Catholics. For other examples, see Wilkes (2001).

Some needs are very personal or family-related. Catholics need support in enriching their marriages, rearing children, and strengthening personal relationships. They want help with problems of divorce and remarriage. They need meaningful communities in which they can forge authentic relationships with other Catholics. They want good religious education for their children. They need people to talk to honestly about their hopes, dreams, frustrations, and worries. When at their best, Catholic parishes are good at meeting such needs.

Other needs are more communal in nature. Laypeople long for opportunities to pursue superordinate goals, goals that bring them together around objectives that transcend personal needs. Group goals allow members to rise above self-interest and work toward some common purpose. Members, of course, must participate in the process of identifying that purpose if they are to "own" it. In some parishes, it might be to participate in an ecumenical coalition attempting to reduce poverty in the area. In others, it might be to help support a mission church in an inner-city neighborhood or in a poor nation. Elsewhere, it might be to support a Catholic school that serves the educational needs of nearby Catholics and non-Catholics. It could be running a soup kitchen or clothes closet for the poor. It might be to reestablish relationships with fallen-away Catholics. Whatever the goal, if it inspires members to rally around a cause that transcends their personal needs, it contributes to community.

Conformity and Autonomy.

Overall, Catholics are not as likely as they once were to grant Church leaders final say; nor are they as likely to agree with Church teachings. They are more inclined to believe they have a personal responsibility to make up their own minds and, while doing so, increasingly distinguish between what they consider to be core beliefs and practices and what they consider peripheral or optional. Catholics are most likely to comply with teachings they consider essential to being Catholic, and they are most likely to express autonomy on matters they consider peripheral. Second, they are most likely to comply in areas where they believe Church leaders have more expertise than other people, and more likely to think autonomously when they believe that they, and others whom they know, have as much expertise as church leaders.

These circumstances help to explain why Catholics agree with Church teachings related to the Trinity, Incarnation, Resurrection, and the Real Presence. People feel these are core issues on which theologians and clergy have more expertise than other people they know. The same circumstances explain why Catholics feel free to disagree with teachings related to birth control, abortion, unions, and the death penalty. They believe these are more peripheral issues on which laypeople have at least as much expertise.

In short, Catholic laypeople no longer grant Church leaders unconditional authority, especially in peripheral areas where they feel other equally credible experts exist. The laity no longer assumes that the magisterium has the sole responsibility for formulating Church teachings or the authority to command compliance with these teachings. The laity grants Church leaders authority in what it considers core areas of faith and morals, but is quite willing to turn to its own experiences and the experiences of other people on other matters.

Thus, as American Catholics have journeyed from the pre–Vatican II era to the post–Vatican II era, two important things have happened. An increasingly educated, post–Vatican II, American laity is deciding what it considers to be the core elements of the Catholic faith; it is not leaving that determination up to the magisterium as much as less educated, pre–Vatican II Catholics once did. It also is limiting the magisterium's authority to what it considers core matters of faith and morals.

This interpretation accounts for the patterns we see in our data. It explains, too, why Church leaders have little or no difficulty producing agreement on some issues (such as the Real Presence) but have much less success producing agreement with the Church's opposition to abortion. It also leads us to predict that Church leaders will have only limited success in their most recent campaign to change Catholics' views on the death penalty unless and until they develop programs that encourage serious discussions that review the gradual evolution of the Church's teaching on this issue.

Our data also suggest that the trend toward autonomy will extend into the future. The inevitable passing of the pre–Vatican II generation, which complies with Church teachings the most, foreshadows a continuing decline in conformity. So does the growing size of the post–Vatican II generation, which is far more autonomous in its approach to faith and morals. The trend will not affect core Church teachings as much as it will the laity's views on issues it considers peripheral, but it will be a persisting challenge to Church leaders in the years ahead.

In our view, Church leaders should respond in three ways. They ought to celebrate the conformity that exists around core issues, where the laity and the magisterium agree that Church leaders have legitimate teaching authority. They need to come to grips with the conditions that foster autonomy, especially on more peripheral matters where laypeople feel they have at least as much authority. And, they should search for ways to increase the laity's agreement with Church teachings. Let's consider each of these courses of action.

In terms of celebration, clergy and laypeople alike should take pride in the fact that Catholic identity and core Catholic beliefs endure. They should rejoice that a majority of Catholics are still registered parishioners, still attend Mass on a regular (though not always weekly) basis, and still marry other Catholics in the Church. They should be proud that the laity has stuck with the Church despite highly embarrassing and very costly cases of immoral conduct by some priests. Both laity and clergy should be overjoyed that the laity has as much confidence as it does in the leadership of the clergy it knows best. They should take pride that Catholics still value and see as closely interrelated the sacraments and the priesthood. They should be pleased that Catholic laypeople express as much interest as they do in participating in parish and diocesan life. They also need to recognize and honor the many other ways that clergy and laypeople act out their faith in their daily lives. Catholics are having an ever-increasing influence on public life in the United States.

At the same time, Church leaders must come to terms with the social conditions that foster disagreement with some Church teachings, especially those that laypeople are most inclined to see as marginal to their identity as Catholics. Today's laypeople are the most highly educated and most resourceful laity in American Catholic church history. They also are fully American and embrace much of American culture. As a result, they have confidence in their own abilities and judgments, which they feel ought to affect their approach to Church teachings. When they distinguish between items they consider to be central to the faith and those they deem peripheral, they are reaching conclusions that Church leaders need to take seriously.

What can Church leaders do to increase agreement with Church teachings? Here we call upon sociological principles to offer three suggestions. First, as we have already suggested, leaders need to build relationships among Catholics. The relationships Catholics have with other Catholics in their families, peer groups, parishes, and parochial schools are the vehicles through which the faith is transmitted and reinforced. The stronger these relationships, the more likely Catholics are to embrace Church teachings.

Second, leaders need to communicate the Church's core values in ways that speak to people's needs. To do that, leaders need to be credible and competent models of the faith. They need to understand the life circumstances and lifestyles of today's Catholics (we hope our research, and the studies done by other researchers, aid in this process). The words and other symbols they use to communicate Church teachings must resonate with the culture. Their explanations of faith and morals should include persuasive evidence that the Church's truth claims are tenable; their arguments should be reasoned and reasonable, and not rely solely on tradition or authority. As much as possible, leaders must see to it that their message is the same in all spheres, such as families, parishes, and parochial schools. They also need to make sure that the Church's core values are clearly expressed in activities ranging from weekend liturgies and classroom assignments to family gatherings and school sporting events.

Finally, leaders need to make the acceptance of church teachings as attractive and rewarding as possible. Agreement with church teachings should be associated with opportunities and benefits that are not available to people who disagree. What should leaders do about non-compliance? In sects and cults, which tend to have exclusive membership policies, leaders are inclined to banish people who dissent from group norms and values. In churches, such as the Roman Catholic Church, leaders are expected to take a more inclusive approach. They should maintain relationships with people who are not ready to embrace Church teachings; listen to their questions, doubts, and concerns;

try to interpret Church teachings in meaningful ways; and strive toward a convergence of views.

We offer these suggestions to catechists, youth ministers, religious educators, and persons in other forms of parish and diocesan ministry. These lay ecclesial ministers have very special opportunities to apply these ideas in their relationships with Catholics of all ages. But these ideas also apply to parents and others who may not be parish or diocesan ministers in the formal sense, but who also can be leaders in passing on the faith. We call special attention to small faith communities, which we believe can play a vital role in forging agreement with Church teachings.

Small groups are a form of community life that is relatively new to American Catholicism. They are growing in every diocese, and some people even see them as a new way of being Church; for example, four million U.S. Catholics have participated in the RENEW movement since 1980. The RENEW program builds groups of eight to ten people who meet for six weeks in Advent and in Lent to become acquainted, to read and discuss the Scriptures, to share their faith, and to support one another. Today, about one million Catholics are members of various kinds of small Christian communities that extend beyond RENEW.

Catholics in small Christian communities take their faith very seriously (their Mass attendance rate is more than twice the national average). They study Church teachings more than most other lay people. They discuss theological and ecclesial issues with their peers. Although they don't always arrive at conclusions that conform to Church teachings, they certainly agree with the Church on matters that are central to the faith. People who belong to these groups also are active members of Catholic parishes. Their close relationship with parishes means they are a leavening influence in the larger Catholic community. Rather than being isolated, sectarian pockets of discontented Catholics, they tend to be just the opposite: parishioners whose extensive ties with other Catholics give them exceptional opportunities to exert an influence that far exceeds their numbers.

Most parish priests, diocesan leaders, and bishops who have encouraged RENEW groups and small Christian communities have seen the benefits these groups can have. Other leaders would be wise to work as closely as possible with these highly committed laypeople. Diocesan and parish leaders might grant members of these communities special opportunities to participate in setting Church policies related to matters such as leadership in priestless parishes. They might welcome members of small Christian communities into consultations on community building and faith sharing, so the lessons learned in the communities might be shared more widely. They might invite members of the communities to share their faith experiences with less active parishioners, in hopes of increasing the latter's involvement in parish life.

Of course, for diocesan and parish leaders to engage small Christian communities in such activities, leaders must build relationships with these communities. They must come to know their members, learn about the communities' previous activities, and determine how much trust they can have in the communities' members. Likewise, members of small faith communities must come to know diocesan and parish leaders, observe the way they exercise and delegate authority, and demonstrate that they have the best interest of the Church at heart. Such relationships take time to build, but they are well worth pursuing.

Variations in Community, Conformity, and Autonomy

Church history also teaches that there are always some people who are more active in community life than others. There are always some who are more likely to stress conformity to Church teachings than others. We offer figure 9.3 as one way to help situate various groups of Catholics along these intersecting axes. The vertical axis runs from high community at the top to low community at the bottom. The horizontal axis runs from conformity at the left to complete autonomy at the right. The intersection of the two axes marks the spot where there is medium community and medium conformity.

We use scores on our index of commitment to the Church as our indicator of involvement in the Catholic community. High scores on the index indicate that Catholics believe the Church is an important part of their life, that they cannot imagine leaving the Church, and that they attend Mass weekly. Low scores indicate that the Church is unimportant to them, that they can imagine circumstances under which they might leave the Church, and they seldom, if ever, attend Mass. Twenty-three percent of Catholics in our 1999 survey were high on commitment (score 3), 60 percent were medium (score 2), and 17 percent were low (score 1). The mean score on this three-point scale was 2.1.

For the horizontal axis, we use responses to our nine questions about what it takes to be a good Catholic. The higher the percentage of Catholics agreeing with traditional Church standards about what it takes to be a good Catholic, the more Catholics tend in the direction of conformity. The lower the percentage agreeing with these standards (and saying that a person can be a good Catholic without conforming to them), the more the group tends toward autonomy. Specifically, we first took a mean of the two items that describe core doctrines (belief in the Resurrection and the Real Presence). That mean score showed that 68 percent of Catholics agreed with these beliefs. We also took a mean of the seven items that fewer than half of Catholics said are key components of being a good Catholic; we called these "peripheral" in chapter 3. That mean score indicates only 34 percent agreement with these Church teachings.

Figure 9.3.   Variations in Community, Conformity, and Autonomy: All Beliefs, 1999

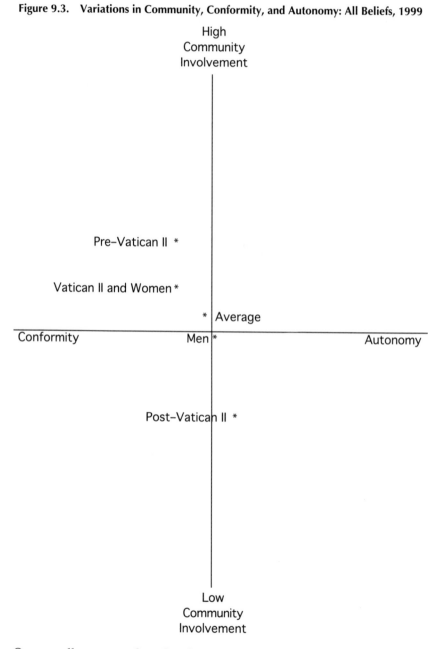

Our overall measure of conformity versus autonomy is the mean of the two measures (the two core items and seven peripheral items). The overall mean score was 51 percent.

With these procedures, we can see where Catholic men and women and the three generations fall on the vertical and horizontal axes in figure 9.3. Pre–Vatican II Catholics are most involved in the Catholic community (mean = 2.3) and most likely to conform to Church teachings (mean = 55 percent). They are followed by women and Vatican II Catholics, both of whom are not quite as involved (mean = 2.1) and are a bit more autonomous in their approach to faith and morals (mean = 53 percent). Next are men, who are even less involved (mean = 2.0) and more autonomous (mean = 49 percent). Post–Vatican II Catholics are least involved in the Catholic community (mean = 1.7) and the most autonomous of all (mean = 47 percent).

Data on how the groups fared on the items they consider core components of Catholic identity and the seven items they consider peripheral reveal another set of important findings. For all groups, the mean scores on the core items tended toward the conformity end of the scale, thereby indicating consensus on central issues of faith. Seventy-one percent of women and Vatican II Catholics agreed with the two core items. So did 67 percent of pre–Vatican II Catholics, 65 percent of post–Vatican II Catholics, and 64 percent of men. On the other hand, mean scores on the periphery items were closer to the autonomy end, thereby indicating a great deal more disagreement on issues that Catholics think are more tangential. Only 42 percent of pre–Vatican II Catholics, 35 percent of Vatican II Catholics, 34 percent of men and women, and 29 percent of post–Vatican II Catholics agreed with the seven periphery items. In short, the gap between official Church teachings and laypeople is much larger on peripheral issues than it is on core issues.

These findings have numerous implications for people ministering to Catholics who differ in gender, generation, and commitment to the Church. Let us explore some of these implications.

Gender Differences

Clergy and lay leaders need to appreciate the similarities and differences between Catholic men and women. We have shown that men and women agree on many core teachings and on the need for laypeople to have a say in parish and diocesan policies. Men and women also respect the efforts parish priests are making on behalf of the Catholic community. Thus, in some areas of ministry the same policies and programs will meet the needs of both men and women. Men and women can share governance responsibilities on parish councils, educational duties in Catholic schools and parish-based catechetical programs, and liturgical roles as Eucharistic ministers and lectors. As members of Bible study and prayer groups, they can be expected to agree more often than they disagree. Small Christian communities provide positive examples of such egalitarian leadership.

Yet, men and women also differ. Women are still more religiously active than men. They feel increasingly alienated from the organizational life of the Church, in part because of the Vatican's views on women's issues. They have more liberal views than men do on issues such as health care for poor children and military spending. Thus, it sometimes makes sense to tailor programs specifically to men and specifically to women.

Some parishes conduct occasional "women's Masses" and get very positive responses from women parishioners. Parishes also might consider offering programs relating to women's career goals and Christian ways of handling obstacles women encounter in the workplace, and forging a relationship between their faith and their roles in the corporate world. Parishes also might try to meet the needs of women parishioners through programs having to do with women's health and family matters. Given women's disproportionate role as caregivers in both their immediate and their extended families, parish-based opportunities for women to share their experiences and draw support from one another seem to be warranted. Also, because women tend to outlive men, parishes might create opportunities for widows to meet or assist in organizing events that link widows socially and spiritually.

Parishes might try to address men's needs as well. Some parishes have histories of offering recreational opportunities through activities such as summer softball teams and occasional golf outings. These are commendable attempts to address men's social interests, but men's concerns extend into other areas as well. Among young adult men, these include the desire to meet women who are comparable in age and similar in faith. Among men in the workplace, there are often moral dilemmas and anxieties related to job security. Men, especially those who travel frequently, face problems related to the amount of time they spend at work and with their families. Retirement from work and men's health issues also cannot be overlooked. Some men have time on their hands and would like to donate their carpentry and electrical skills to their parishes. Others would be willing to contribute their talents in areas such as long-range planning and program evaluation. All of these represent fertile grounds for building relationships among men and helping men link faith with other aspects of their lives.

Gender also affects Catholics' participation in the central operations of the Church. In today's world, if any organization, secular or religious, is to enjoy the full support of its members, its members must feel a genuine sense of ownership. Similarly, if today's Church is to be an authentic expression of all its members, women's voices as well as men's need to be heard. Women as well as men need to participate in decisions that are made at all levels of Church life. Women as well as men need confidence that their concerns will be reflected in Church policies and ceremonies.

The Church is making important strides in these directions, as evidenced by the large percentage of lay ecclesial ministers who are women. These strides have quite dramatically increased women's access to influence (the ability to have an impact, even when opposed). They have not been as effective in increasing women's access to authority (the legitimate right to command others). Given our evidence that women are as likely as men to favor democratic decision making, the gap in women's access to positions of authority will continue to be a flash point in the Church.

This flash point cannot be overlooked. Historically, women have been willing to provide many services for the Church. They have encouraged their sons to consider the priesthood and their daughters to consider the sisterhood. They have prepared meals for funerals, washed and ironed linens for the altar, and helped their children with their Sunday school lessons. They have done these things freely, and often without much recognition, because they have been committed to the Church. Our data, along with data from other research, clearly indicate, however, that women's attachment to the Church is declining. This decline is the result of many forces in society as well as in the Church, including women's perception that their gifts are often overutilized but undervalued.

How, then, should Church leaders respond? They need to ask questions of women and listen to what they have to say. Unless leaders listen to women's concerns and address the conditions underlying them, the risk will be that women's alienation from the Church will turn to indifference and even lower levels of participation. Losing the support of women would be a major setback for the Church.

With the large percentage of lay ministers who are women, it also is important to pay attention to the way men perceive and respond to Church leadership. Some men need to adjust to having women in positions of authority. Others may have concerns about their place in parish and diocesan leadership positions that are largely in the hands of women. Just as some women historically have been reluctant to step forward because they saw the Church as "a man's world," so too some men may be reluctant to participate in what they consider to be "a woman's world." To the extent that such responses go undetected, and the signals may be quite subtle and hard to read at times, they can lead to unwanted alienation and reduced levels of community participation.

Generational Differences.

There is a difference between the effects of age and the effects of generation on people's religious beliefs and practices. Research clearly shows that age has its own effects. People tend to be religious when they are young and under the supervision of their parents. When they reach their teenage and young adult years, during which they tend to be single and the culture gives them permission to experiment with new ideas (including the idea of not being actively religious), their involvement declines. When they marry, and especially when they have children of their own, they tend to return to Church.

While valid, this perspective is incomplete. It overlooks the fact that people are born at different periods of time, periods that are often quite different economically, politically, and culturally. Some people grew up in the Great Depression of the 1930s; others in the economic prosperity of the 1990s. Some grew up in political liberalism of the 1960s, others in the political conservatism of the 1980s. Some grew up in the Catholic ghetto of the pre–Vatican II years, others in the ecumenical age of the post–Vatican II years. Thus, the experiences people have during their formative years (from about eleven to twenty-three years of age) are likely to be very different. The experiences undergone in the formative years also have long-lasting effects on people's religious beliefs and practices. The pre–Vatican II Church's emphasis on being the "one true Church" and its insistence on conformity with Church teachings produced high levels of commitment that persist among older Catholics. The post–Vatican II Church's more ecumenical and personal approach to faith has led to lower levels of commitment that are likely to persist throughout the lives of today's young Catholics. When they marry and have children, they are not as likely to rebound into the Church as their parents and grandparents did. When they are in their forties and fifties, they are not as likely to feel a need to support the Church financially. When they reach their sixties and seventies, they also will not be as attached to parishes and dioceses.

Thus, in addition to ministries based on the age model, we also need ministries that are based on the generation model. These include ministries targeted at the social and spiritual needs of each generation, and ministries that build cross-generational relationships. Generation-based ministries can have transformative effects. As evidence, we offer a true story about a woman who belongs to the Vatican II generation. She is actively involved in parish ministry, and has three post–Vatican II sons. She was enrolled in a one-week pastoral institute taught by one of the coauthors. She was troubled by the fact that her boys (in their late teens and twenties) were not as religiously active as she would like them to be. She felt guilty, wondering where she and her husband had gone wrong. Her instructor asked her to read some of the research on generations and to apply it to her own life. She did, asking her sons the survey questions and using the same response categories she had found in one of the books. Here is what she reported in one part of the course paper:

> Although they went to Mass and received Communion at least once a week and prayed more than once a week when they were growing up, but now only go to Mass

and receive Holy Communion once a month, all three of my X Generation sons see themselves as fairly religious. They all still pray more than once a week, although this never includes the rosary and for two of them devotions to Mary or a special saint. My son the police officer has special devotion to St. Christopher. (I didn't have the heart to tell him about St. Christopher.) They seldom, if ever, read the Bible and never attend Bible study or prayer groups.

Belief in the Trinity and transubstantiation is somewhat important to them, while Jesus' resurrection and incarnation is very important. Two of them disagree that the Pope is the Vicar of Christ and that the Catholic Church is the one true church but agree that it is important to obey Church teachings.

They all agree that one can be a good Catholic without going to Mass and that women should be allowed to be priests. They all think that the use of birth control and premarital sex should be up to the individual. Abortion is wrong for two of them and wrong except under certain circumstances for one of them. They answered the same way for homosexual acts.

All three of my sons have sensed the presence of God in a special way many times. The two older sons said God has taken care of them when they really needed him many times and forgiven them as often.

My oldest son has heard, talked about, and read about Vatican II a few times. My other two sons have had no experience with it.

While all disagree somewhat that there is something very special about being a Catholic, which you can't find in other religions, they all agree, and two strongly, that being Catholic has given them a solid moral foundation.

Two sons agree that they could be happy in some other church but cannot imagine themselves being anything other than Catholic. None donate either their time or fair share of money to the Church.

Well, I didn't hear all the answers I would have liked to have heard, but, on the other hand, I wasn't totally surprised after reading *The Search for Common Ground*, taking this course, and doing research for this paper. My sons are post–Vatican II; they are the X Generation. Their formation took place in a different time than mine. Their theology is part of their pop culture, their dress, their films and music videos, and cyberspace, all of which I now better understand. . . . I have learned that there is more of the Catholic faith in them than I expected. Most importantly, what I have learned from this study is not how to fight them to accept my beliefs and practices but to accept them, to use Paul Wilkes' expression, as "good enough Catholics."

You can almost hear this mother's sigh of relief. She understands herself and her children more than she did before. Her newfound generational perspective has contributed to her self-confidence and improved her relationships with her sons.

Part of the challenge in today's Church is for pre–Vatican II and Vatican II Catholics to understand post–Vatican II Catholics, and to make room in the Church for them. Older generations of Catholics often feel that liturgies and homilies should meet their needs and appeal to their sense of what is truly Catholic music. They often feel that they are entitled to leadership roles in the Church because of their age, experience, and years of support. They sometimes have unflattering images of the post–Vatican II generation. All of these conditions produce barriers that limit young people's involvement in parish and diocesan ministry.

Conversely, young Catholics also should seize the opportunities that are already there for them to stake a claim in the Church. Many pre–Vatican II and Vatican II Catholics wish that more young people would volunteer for leadership roles. They are excited when they see young adults at local, regional, and national Church meetings. They respond positively when young people accept invitations to participate in parish and diocesan activities. But many post–Vatican II Catholics who have much to offer the Church do not take advantage of these opportunities. Many who say they want more democratic decision making in the Church choose not to participate. Church leaders and young adults need to identify the circumstances that keep some young people from accepting responsibility for the future of the Church. Then they need to address the circumstances.

Commitment to the Church

Just as Church leaders are being challenged to minister to both men and women, and different generations, they also are being challenged to reach out to Catholics who have different levels of attachment to the Church. After the scandals that have rocked the Church, and the cultural forces that have pulled many people away from it, many Catholics remain steadfastly attached to the Church. These people should be appreciated, and this appreciation should be expressed in every way possible.

The more pressing concern, of course, is how to reach and minister to the Catholics who still think of themselves as Catholic but have fewer connections with the Church. This group includes nonparishioners as well as people who belong to parishes but do not think of them as being a very important part of their life. Research also has shown that these Catholics are more likely to be black or Hispanic than white; divorced or single (never married) rather than married; married to a non-Catholic instead of a Catholic; and young rather than old. If reintegrating these groups into the Catholic community is a goal, the question is how to do it.

We conclude with three suggestions. First, the best way to establish contact with Catholics who are low in commitment is through people who share their age, marital status, and race or ethnicity but who remain committed to the Church. Young blacks who are active in the Church have a better chance than older whites do to interact freely with young African–Americans who are disconnected from the Church. Divorced Catholics who are still active in parish life have more natural lines of contact with divorced Catholics who have fallen away from the Church. Attempts to evangelize Catholics who are low in commitment should follow these natural lines of social interaction. Attempts to reach out across racial, ethnic, age, and marital lines (e.g., asking retired white men to evangelize young African–American men) are not as productive.

Second, we should not present Catholics with prospects that are incompatible with today's social conditions. Some Catholics believe the Church should return to a pre–Vatican II way of "being Church" and that those who don't approve should leave. We do not endorse this approach. After all, sociological and theological conditions that produced the pre–Vatican II way of life have disappeared. Others suggest that we reassert the authority of the Church hierarchy and resist attempts to democratize the Church. This option misunderstands the laity's willingness to participate and runs the risk of driving the least committed Catholics completely out of the Church and into the welcoming arms of other religious traditions.

Finally, we suggest that leaders present the least committed with a new way of "being Church," one that draws on the best elements in the Catholic tradition and meets the needs of today's Catholics. Leaders should present them with a Catholic Church that includes specifically Catholic ways of life but is also ecumenical. They should offer them specifically Catholic beliefs (e.g., the Real Presence) but also beliefs Catholics have in common with other Christian faiths (e.g., belief in the Trinity). Catholics should express pride in being Catholic, without expressing antipathy toward people who belong to other religious traditions. Catholic identity should present a clear sense of what makes the Catholic faith unique, but it also must indicate what Catholics share with other Christians. Church leaders should communicate that being Catholic includes a sense of obligation to the Catholic community but also is freely chosen. They should offer a Church that includes a willingness to sacrifice for the well-being of the whole but also addresses Catholics' personal needs and interests. They should stress respect for both the Church's hierarchical heritage and its identity as the "people of God." They need to find ways for the magisterium and the laity to work together in formulating policies that reflect the will of God and the best instincts of God's people. Given commitment's importance for virtually all beliefs and practices, cultivating commitment should be a top priority in the years to come.

Appendix A

Race and Ethnicity among Catholics: Do They Make a Difference?

At the beginning of the twenty-first century, American Catholics are more racially diverse than ever. This presents a challenge to the leadership, because maintaining goodwill and unity in the future will be difficult. The majority of Catholics today are the descendants of European immigrants from Ireland, Germany, Italy, Poland, and other nations. The largest minority is the Latinos, estimated to be 20 to 30 percent of the total in the year 2000. Because of rapid immigration and high fertility, Latinos are increasing year by year. Latino Catholics belong to distinct national groups, the largest of which is Mexican (about 64 percent of all the Latinos), then Puerto Rican (11 percent), Cuban (5 percent), and Central/South American (13 percent); the rest are from other nations and Spain (Diaz-Stevens and Stevens-Arroyo, 1998: 17). Two other minority groups are African Americans (about 3 or 4 percent of all Catholics) and Asian Americans (about 2 or 3 percent). Asian Americans, like Latinos, are growing in numbers year by year.

How different are these groups? Racial differences are difficult to describe reliably if the group in question is small, because nationwide polls include too few cases to allow any conclusions. Only in the case of Latino Catholics do we have good survey data showing how they are distinctive.

Latinos

Table A.1 shows Latino versus non-Latino differences in our 1999 survey. Questions on which they did not differ are shown with asterisks. For simplicity, the non-Latinos are labeled "Europeans," even though they include small numbers of African Americans and Asian Americans.

The differences in table A.1 are the largest we found; on many other topics

151

Table A.1. Comparison of Latino and European Catholics, 1999

	Latinos %	Europeans %
Age 34 or younger	48	33
College graduates	12	25
Now registered members of a parish	54	70
Mass attendance weekly or more often	31	39
Who should have the final say about what is right or wrong regarding these topics? (percent saying "Church leaders")		
A divorced Catholic re-marrying without getting an annulment	*	*
A Catholic practicing contraceptive birth control	5	13
A Catholic advocating free choice regarding abortion	10	22
A Catholic who engages in homosexual behavior	*	*
Sexual relations outside of marriage	13	27
Favor more democratic decision making in Church affairs		
that do not involve matters of faith, at the local parish level	60	67
At the diocese level	44	63
At the level of the Vatican	45	56
Agree: Laity should have the right to participate in:		
Deciding how parish income should be spent	77	84
Selecting the priests for their parish	*	*
Deciding whether women should be ordained to the priesthood	*	*

* = The difference is too small to be significant at .05, thus not shown. Percentages for the entire sample are found in chapters 4 and 8.

the Latinos and Europeans did not differ, and those topics include how important specific elements of Catholicism are to the respondents: sacraments, church involvement in social justice, spirituality, and Vatican authority. Latinos and Europeans did not differ on whether Catholicism contains a greater share of truth than other religions; on ratings of priests and parish life; on the question of priestly celibacy; and on what the requirements are to be a "good Catholic." In summary: the main differences are slightly less acceptance by Latinos of the authority of Church leaders in matters of sexuality and reproduction and slightly less support for greater lay participation in church decision making.

We can get more information from the 1995 survey of Catholics by Davidson et al. (1997). Table A.2 compares Latinos and Europeans in that survey. (The "European" category does not include African Americans or Asian Americans.)

The Latinos interviewed in the 1995 survey were more educated than average Latinos; 20 percent said they were college graduates, and this compares with 9 percent of all Latinos in 1991, according to U.S. census data. The higher percentage in the sample may be a product of the interview method (by phone).

We see in the table that these Latinos do not differ from European Catholics in frequency of Mass attendance or in use of the rosary, but they practice more private devotions to Mary or a special saint, and they go more frequently to

Table A.2. Comparison of Latino and European Catholics, Nationwide, 1995

	Latinos %	Europeans %
50 years old or younger	84	67
College graduate	20	30
Practices:		
Mass attendance weekly or more often	*	*
Pray the rosary weekly or more often	*	*
Practice devotions to Mary or a special saint weekly or more often	41	27
Go to private confession with a priest regularly or sometimes	26	18
Attitudes:		
The Church should put more emphasis on traditional teachings. Agree	73	60
The Pope is the Vicar of Christ on earth. Agree	*	*
Laypeople are just as important a part of the Church as priests are. Agree	76	85
It's important to obey church teachings even if I don't understand them. Agree	52	44
My parish is an important part of my life. Agree	83	72

* = Difference is too small to be significant at .05, hence not shown.

private confession with a priest. In attitudes toward the Church they are more traditional than European Catholics, and they rate their parishes as more important in their lives than do Europeans.

On numerous other topics the Latinos and Europeans agree. They agree on topics of sexual morality, such as contraception and premarital sex (a minority says each is always or usually wrong). They agree (two-thirds) on the specialness of Catholicism as opposed to other churches. They agree in their ratings of how good their parishes are. They have the same level of agreement (about half) that Catholics have a duty to try to close the gap between rich and poor. They agree on their self-estimates of how religious they are now. The overall picture is a moderate level of disagreement on a limited number of Church issues, alongside agreement on others.

A 1997 survey of young adult Catholics done by Hoge et al. (2001) provides additional information. This survey included Catholics 20 to 39 years old who had been confirmed during their adolescent years; therefore, the sample has a disproportionate number of Catholics who have been churchgoing since youth. It found a limited number of differences between Latinos and all others. As in the other surveys, the similarities were greater than the differences, yet five significant differences occurred:

First, the Latinos reported greater participation in personal devotions of many kinds, including making the Stations of the Cross, saying the rosary, wearing medals and scapulars, keeping images of saints in the home, having altars in the home, having a car or home blessed, and carrying out *promesas* (promises) in return for divine favors. They were also more constant in prayer.

Second, Latinos had more close friends in their parishes than the others. Also they made more positive evaluations of their parishes, and they were more hesitant about increased democracy in parish decision making.

Third, Latinos more often agreed that "the Catholic Church is the one true Church" (64 percent versus 48 percent of the non-Latinos) and that "the only absolute Truth for humankind is in the teachings of Jesus Christ" (87 percent versus 73 percent).

Fourth, Latinos agreed more than others that Catholics have a duty to try to close the gap between the rich and the poor and to try to preserve the environment.

Fifth, Latinos were less informed about the institutional Church, as indicated by the number who had heard of the Second Vatican Council (27 percent versus 56 percent).

By contrast, in the 1997 survey, Latinos were *not* more likely to shift from Catholicism to other denominations than other Catholics. In spite of numerous reports of many Latino Catholics switching to Protestant groups today, the proportion of Latinos doing this was not greater than that of other Catholics.

Several good studies of Latino Catholics provide information on how they are unique (see Deck 1989; Diaz-Stevens and Stevens-Arroyo 1998). For example, it has been repeatedly found that Latinos are relatively less involved than other Catholics in parish life, but they are more active in personal devotions and family devotions. Family life is stronger among Latinos than among other Catholics. Women (Latinas) are more active in parish life and devotional life than Latino men, and commonly religion is defined among Latinos as being the women's domain.

From census data we know that Latinos are more urbanized than other Americans, and they are concentrated in just a few parts of the United States. Five states contain the vast majority—California, Texas, New York, Florida, and Illinois. Also Latinos readily intermarry with non-Latinos, so within one or two generations the boundaries of the Latino community become blurry.

African–Americans

Survey research on African–American Catholics is sparse. The best data we know are from the General Social Survey, a nationwide survey done annually since 1972. Table A.3 shows five questions asked repeatedly from 1983 to 1998.

Compared with European Catholics, African American Catholics attend

Table A.3. Responses of European Catholics, African American Catholics, and Asian American Catholics, 1983 to 1998

	Euro-pean %	African American %	Asian American %
Would you call yourself a strong Catholic? Yes	40	33	47
How often do you attend religious services?			
Weekly or more	39	24	45
How often do you pray? Daily or more	56	61	57
The Bible: It is the actual Word of God, or it is the inspired Word of God, but not everything should be taken literally.	84	84	80
How much confidence do you have in the people running these institutions: Organized religion? A great deal	34	27	*

* = not enough cases. On the other questions the number of African Americans is 398 or more and the number of Asian Americans is 75 or more.

Mass less regularly, see themselves less as being "strong Catholics," and have less confidence in the people running organized religion. Other differences are small. Unfortunately, we know of no research that asked large numbers of different racial groups questions about religion and the Church.

A few studies have been done specifically of African American Catholics, but their findings are not totally consistent. Cavendish and his associates (1998) found that black Catholics have higher levels of private religious devotions and more frequent spiritual experiences than white Catholics. Also black Catholics tend to be traditional in worship and liturgical preference. Black Catholic parishes sponsor more social action and community service programs than other parishes (Cavendish, 2000). Taylor and his associates (1996) found that black Methodists, Baptists, and Catholics attend church more often than whites. Blacks have higher levels of self-reported importance of religion in their lives than do other groups, and they engage in more private religious behavior such as reading religious materials. Feigelman and his collaborators (1991) had different findings; they discovered that black Catholics attend Mass less than white Catholics do and have higher rates of interfaith marriage. These research studies are based on limited surveys or on reports by pastors, hence are not as reliable and generalizable as we would like.

Asian Americans

Table A.3 shows that Asian American Catholics attend Mass more often than other Catholics, and they consider themselves stronger Catholics than other

Catholics do. Other research has told us that Asian American Catholics are found especially in the West Coast area. Davidson et al.'s (1997) national survey found that Asian American Catholics scored higher than any other racial group on an index of traditional beliefs (such as Incarnation and the importance of obeying Church teachings) and practices (such as Mass attendance and praying the rosary). They are also the least likely to disagree with the Church's views on the importance of attending Mass and limiting ordination to celibate men. They, along with Latinos, are more likely than other Catholics to participate in Scripture-oriented devotional practices such as reading the Bible, and they agree more than other Catholics with the Church's teachings on sexuality and reproduction. On the other hand, they are not as likely as other Catholics to agree with its social teachings. These findings are tentative because they are based on a small sample, but they are consistent with reports we received from parish and diocesan leaders who minister to Asian American Catholics. They need further testing.

Appendix B

Registered Parish Members Compared with Other Catholics

Throughout this book we have shown that three characteristics influence Catholics' attitudes on Church-related issues: their level of commitment to the Catholic religion, their generation, and their gender. A fourth characteristic is also important, but we did not include it in the book to avoid complexity. It is whether the person is a registered member of his or her parish.

Past polls have found that about 70 percent of all baptized Catholic adults are registered in some parish. The 1995 survey by Davidson and his associates found 69 percent. In our 1999 survey, the figure was 67 percent. Parish members are more likely to be women than men, more likely to be older, more likely to be currently married, much more likely to have a spouse who is Catholic, and more than twice as likely to be in a marriage approved by the Church.

Catholics who are registered in a parish are more likely than nonparishioners to support the institutional Church and its teachings (see table B.1). The registered and nonregistered parishioners are different. The table tells us that the biggest differences are that the former attend Mass more often, see the Church as more important in their lives, and insist that belief in the Real Presence is essential for one to be a good Catholic.

Registered Catholics are no different from nonregistered Catholics in two respects. The two groups agree in their views that laity should participate in decisions about parish income, and they agree in favoring more democratic decision making at the level of the parish, the diocese, and the Vatican. (The data on decision making are not shown in the table.) We can probably summarize that registration status has little to do with attitudes on parish governance; both groups favor lay involvement.

No one should believe that being registered in a parish *causes* the distinc-

Table B.1. Behaviors and Attitudes of Registered and Unregistered Parishioners

	Registered Parishioner %	Not Registered Parishioner %
Demographic Characteristics:		
Female	55	41
Older than 50	38	20
Behavior and Attitudes:		
Attend Mass at least weekly	51	10
Pray daily or more often	78	55
Agree: The Catholic Church is one of the most important influences in my life.	54	24
Agree: Parish priests today are doing a good job.	92	85
Agree: Most priests don't expect the lay members to be leaders, just followers.	42	51
Agree: Catholic parishes are too big and impersonal.	40	58
Agree: Catholicism contains a greater share of truth than other religions do.	62	47
Agree: It would be good if married men could be ordained as priests.	72	88
Agree: It would be good if married women could be ordained as priests.	45	69
Agree: You can be a good Catholic without		
Obeying Church teachings on birth control	66	83
Obeying Church teachings on divorce and remarriage	61	71
Obeying Church teachings on abortion	49	60
Having one's marriage approved by the Church	63	76
Donating time or money for the poor	52	63
Believing in the Real Presence of Jesus in the Eucharist	29	56
Believing in the resurrection of Jesus	18	35
Agree: Laity should have the right to participate in		
Deciding how parish income should be spent.	*	*
Selecting priests for parishes.	68	81
Deciding whether women should be ordained to the priesthood.	58	73

* = Difference is too small to be significant at .05, thus not shown.

tive behaviors and attitudes shown in the table. The data do not tell us whether parish membership is a source of the high involvement and loyalty or whether Catholics join a parish because they are already involved and committed. Probably there is a reciprocal effect of each on the other. The value of table B.1 is that it answers the simple question of whether registered parishioners are (for whatever reason) different from the nonregistered. The answer is yes, in many ways: registered Catholics attend Mass much more often, are more devotional, like their priests and parishes more, and are less enthusiastic about institutional innovations.

Appendix C

Appendix C.4.1 Types of Marriage by Gender, 1999

	Men %	Women %
Entire sample		
Intrafaith		
Purely	60	51
Currently	12	16
Interfaith		
Purely	25	30
Currently	3	2
Each type		
Intrafaith		
In the Church	81	84
Outside the Church	19	16
Interfaith		
In the Church	35	47
Outside the Church	65	53
Each subtype		
Purely Intrafaith		
In the Church	82	85
Outside the Church	18	14
Currently Intrafaith		
In the Church	77	79
Outside the Church	23	21
Purely Interfaith		
In the Church	38	48
Outside the Church	62	52
Currently Interfaith		
In the Church	15	38
Outside the Church	85	62

Appendix C.4.2   Types of Marriage and Commitment to the Church, 1999 (percent)

	Purely Intrafaith		Currently Intrafaith		Purely Interfaith		Currently Interfaith	
	In %	Out %	In %	Out %	In %	Out %	In %	Out %
Commitment								
High	35	11	40	23	24	9	8	0
Medium	54	64	57	73	61	51	92	100
Low	11	26	4	5	14	40	0	0

	Commitment		
	Low %	Medium %	High %
Purely Intrafaith			
In the Church	68	81	94
Outside the Church	32	18	6
Currently Intrafaith			
In the Church	74	74	86
Outside the Church	26	26	14
Purely Interfaith			
In the Church	22	48	68
Outside the Church	78	52	32
Currently Interfaith			
In the Church	0	24	*
Outside the Church	0	76	*

* Not enough cases to compute stable percentages.

Table C. 5.1   Locus of Moral Authority on Five Issues, 1987, 1993, and 1999, by Generations (in percent)

| | Church Leaders | | | | | | | | |
| | Pre-Vatican II | | | Vatican II | | | Post-Vatican II | | |
	1987	1993	1999	1987	1993	1999	1987	1993	1999
A divorced Catholic remarrying without getting an annulment	37	29	27	21	22	23	17	21	14
A Catholic practicing contraceptive birth control	23	24	21	11	12	13	9	9	6
A Catholic advocating free choice regarding abortion	42	32	29	28	19	27	24	16	10
A Catholic who engages in homosexual behavior	46	33	35	32	26	23	26	25	13
Nonmarital sexual relations	47	36	37	28	21	27	23	19	14
	Individuals								
A divorced Catholic remarrying without getting an annulment	25	32	41	30	40	45	33	42	48
A Catholic practicing contraceptive birth control	46	49	55	62	61	62	69	64	66
A Catholic advocating free choice regarding abortion	34	38	39	48	45	47	48	50	52
A Catholic who engages in homosexual behavior	18	29	36	40	44	48	47	48	56
Nonmarital sexual relations	27	36	39	43	44	45	48	52	51
	Both								
A divorced Catholic remarrying without getting an annulment	32	39	30	46	38	32	46	37	35
A Catholic practicing contraceptive birth control	24	27	24	25	27	23	21	27	25
A Catholic advocating free choice regarding abortion	16	29	28	19	36	24	26	34	35
A Catholic who engages in homosexual behavior	21	39	24	15	30	26	21	27	27
Nonmarital sexual relations	16	28	21	15	35	25	26	29	30

Table C.5.2   Locus of Moral Authority on Five Issues, 1987, 1993, and 1999, by High-Commitment Catholics

Percent of Most Highly Committed Catholics Who Look to Church Leaders	1987	1993	1999
A divorced Catholic remarrying without getting an annulment	35	36	42
A Catholic practicing contraceptive birth control	23	24	33
A Catholic advocating free choice regarding abortion	53	36	44
A Catholic who engages in homosexual behavior	52	37	44
Nonmarital sexual relations	54	39	47

Percent of Most Highly Committed Catholics Who Look to the Individual			
A divorced Catholic remarrying without getting an annulment	21	24	22
A Catholic practicing contraceptive birth control	52	48	41
A Catholic advocating free choice regarding abortion	31	32	26
A Catholic who engages in homosexual behavior	30	33	29
Nonmarital sexual relations	29	37	26

Percent of Most Highly Committed Catholics Who Look to Both			
A divorced Catholic remarrying without getting an annulment	44	39	36
A Catholic practicing contraceptive birth control	25	29	26
A Catholic advocating free choice regarding abortion	16	32	30
A Catholic who engages in homosexual behavior	18	30	27
Nonmarital sexual relations	17	24	26

References

Abbott, Walter M. 1966. *The Documents of Vatican II.* New York: Herder and Herder.

Administrative Board of the United States Catholic Conference. 1976. *Political Responsibility: Reflections on an Election Year,* Washington, D.C., 12 February.

————. 1984. *Nuclear War and Peace,* Washington, D.C.

————. 1986. *Economic Justice for All,* Washington, D.C.

————. 1996. *Political Responsibility: Reflection on the 1996 Election Year,* Washington, D.C.

————. 1996. *Political Responsibility: Proclaiming the Gospel of Life, Protecting the Least Among Us, and Pursuing the Common Good,* Washington, D.C.

Albom, Mitch. 1997. *Tuesdays with Morrie.* Garden City, N.Y.: Doubleday.

Allen, Vernon L., David A. Wilder, and Michael L. Atkinson. 1983. Multiple Group Membership and Social Identity. Chap. 5 in *Studies in Social Identity,* edited by Theodore Sarbin and Karl Scheibe. New York: Praeger.

Allitt, Patrick. 1993. *Catholic Intellectuals and Conservative Politics in America, 1950–1985.* Ithaca, N.Y.: Cornell University Press.

Aquinas, St. Thomas. 1947. *Summa Theologica,* Vol. II. New York: Benziger.

Bagley, Ron, and John Roberto. 1996. *Ministry with Young Adults: A National Catholic Initiative.* Washington D.C.: Catholic Campus Ministry Association.

Barna, George. 1991. *What Americans Believe.* Ventura, Calif.: Regal Books.

Barnhart, Heather. 2000. Students Protest Minister's Removal. *National Catholic Reporter,* 28 April, 6.

Bellah, Robert, Richard Madsen, William M. Sullivan, Ann Swidler, and Steven M. Tipton. 1985. *Habits of the Heart.* Berkeley: University of California Press.

Bianchi, Eugene, and Rosemary Ruether. 1992. *A Democratic Catholic Church.* New York: Crossroad.

Briefs: Bishop Says Catholics Get 'D" in Social Teaching. 2000. *National Catholic Reporter,* 28 April, 8.

Brokaw, Tom. 1998. *The Greatest Generation*, New York: Random House.

Bultena, Louis. 1949. Church Membership and Church Attendance, in Madison, Wisconsin. *American Sociological Review* 14: 348–89.

Burns, Gene. 1992. *The Frontiers of Catholicism: The Politics of Ideology in the Liberal World*. Berkeley: University of California Press.

Carey, Ann. 1995. Confused about Changes in the Liturgy? Join the Club. *Our Sunday Visitor*, 24 September.

Catechism of the Catholic Church. 1995. New York: Doubleday.

Cavendish, James C. 2000. Church-Based Community Activism: A Comparison of Black and White Catholic Congregations. *Journal for the Scientific Study of Religion* 39:64–77.

Cavendish, James C., Michael E. Welch, and David C. Leege. 1998. Social Theory and Predictors of Religiosity for Black and White Catholics: Evidence of a 'Black Sacred Cosmos'? *Journal for the Scientific Study of Religion* 37:397–410.

Chaves, Mark, and James C. Cavendish. 1994. More Evidence on U.S. Catholic Church Attendance. *Journal for the Scientific Study of Religion* 33 (December): 376–81.

Christiano, Kevin J. 1991. The Church and the New Immigrants. In *Vatican II and U.S. Catholicism,* edited by Helen Rose Ebaugh. Greenwich, Conn.: JAI Press.

Cogley, John, and Rodger Van Allen. 1986. *Catholic America*. Expanded and updated. Kansas City, Mo.: Sheed & Ward.

Cozzens, Donald B. 2000. *The Changing Face of the Priesthood*. Collegeville, Minn.: Liturgical Press.

The Crisis of Liberal Catholicism. 1999. *Commonweal,* 19 November, seventy-fifth anniversary issue.

D'Antonio, William, V. 1966. The Layman in the Wake of Vatican II. *Ave Maria,* Lenten series, 10–14.

———. 1999a. Latino Catholics: How Different? *National Catholic Reporter,* 29 October, 19.

———. 1999b. Parish Catholics: It Makes a Difference. *National Catholic Reporter,* 29 October, 16.

D'Antonio, William, James Davidson, Dean Hoge, and Ruth Wallace. 1989. *American Catholic Laity in a Changing Church*. Kansas City, Mo.: Sheed & Ward.

———. 1996. *Laity, American and Catholic*. Kansas City, Mo.: Sheed & Ward.

Davidson, James D. 1999a. Division into Two Cultures Not the Whole Picture. *The Catholic Moment,* 24 October, 4.

———. 1999b. Outside the Church: Whom Catholics Marry and Where. *Commonweal,* 10 September, 14–16.

———. 2000. The Search for Common Ground: Three Generations of American Catholics. *Liguorian,* January, 12–16.

Davidson, James D., Alan K. Mock, and C. Lincoln Johnson. 1997. Through the Eye of a Needle: Social Ministry in Affluent Churches. *Review of Religious Research,* March, 247–62.

Davidson, James D., Ralph R. Pyle, and David Reyes. 1995. Persistence and Change in the Protestant Establishment, 1930–1992. *Social Forces,* September, 157–75.

Davidson, James D., Andrea S. Williams, Richard A. Lamanna, Jan Stenftenagel, Kathleen Weigert, William Whalen, and Patricia Wittberg. 1997. *The Search for Common Ground: What Unites and Divides Catholic Americans*. Huntington, Ind.: Our Sunday Visitor.

Deck, Allan Figueroa, S.J. 1989. *The Second Wave: Hispanic Ministry and the Evangelization of Cultures.* New York: Paulist Press.

DeRego, Frank R., and James D. Davidson. 1998. Catholic Deacons: A Lesson in Role Conflict and Ambiguity. In *Religion in a Changing World,* edited by Madeleine Cousineau. New York: Praeger.

Dershowitz, Alan M. 1997. *The Vanishing American Jew.* New York: Simon and Schuster.

Diaz–Stevens, Ana Maria, and Anthony M. Stevens–Arroyo. 1998. *Recognizing the Latino Resurgence in U.S. Religion.* Boulder, Colo.: Westview Press.

Dillon, Michele. 1999. *Catholic Identity.* New York: Cambridge University Press.

DiMaggio, Paul, John Evans, and Bethany Bryson. 1996. Have American Social Attitudes Become More Polarized? *American Journal of Sociology* 102:690–755.

Dinges, William, Dean R. Hoge, Mary Johnson, and Juan L. Gonzales Jr. 1998. A Faith Loosely Held: The Institutional Allegiance of Young Catholics. *Commonweal,* 17 July, 13–18.

Dolan, Jay. 1985. *The American Catholic Experience.* Garden City, N.Y.: Image Books.

Douglass, R. Bruce, and David Hollenbach, eds. 1994. *Catholicism and Liberalism.* New York: Cambridge University Press.

Dulles, Avery, S. J. 1998. Orthodoxy and Social Change. *America,* 20 June, 8–17.

Ebaugh, Helen Rose. 1991. *Vatican II and U.S. Catholicism.* Greenwich, Conn.: JAI Press.

Eckstrom, Kevin. 2000. L.A. Cardinal Calls for "Moral Revolution" Against Death Penalty. *Religion News Service,* 25 May.

Erikson, Erik H. 1968. *Identity: Youth and Crisis.* New York: Norton.

Feigelman, William, Bernard S. Gorman, and Joseph A. Varacalli. 1991. The Social Characteristics of Black Catholics. *Sociology and Social Research* 75:133–43.

Fichter, Joseph. 1951. *Dynamics of a City Church.* Chicago: University of Chicago Press.

———. 1974. *Organization Man in the Church.* Cambridge, Mass.: Schenkman.

———. 1977. Reconstructing Catholicism. *Sociological Analysis* 38:2, 154–64.

Fitzpatrick, Joseph. 1971. *Puerto Rican Americans.* Upper Saddle River, N.J.: Prentice–Hall.

Flannery, Austin, ed. 1992. *Vatican Council II: The Conciliar and Post-Conciliar Documents.* Vols. I and II. Grand Rapids, Mich.: William B. Eerdmans Publishing Company.

Fox, Thomas C. 1995. *Sexuality and Catholicism.* New York: George Braziller.

Fox, Zeni. 1997. *New Ecclesial Ministry.* Kansas City, Mo.: Sheed and Ward.

Froehle, Bryan T., and Mary L. Gautier. 2000. *Catholicism USA.* Maryknoll, N.Y.: Orbis Books.

Gallup Organization. Poll Release: Little Evidence That Born-Again or Conservative Protestants Are More Anti-Catholic Than Are Other Americans. http://www.gallup.com 27 March 2000.

Gallup, George Jr., and Jim Castelli. 1987. *The American Catholic People: Their Beliefs, Practices, and Values.* Garden City, N.Y.: Doubleday and Company.

Gallup, George C., and C. Michael Lindsey. 1999. *Surveying the Religious Landscape.* Harrisburg, Pa.: Morehouse.

Gillis, Chester. 1999. *Roman Catholicism in America.* New York: Columbia University Press.

Gleason, Phillip. 1994. American Catholicism and Liberalism. In *Catholicism and Liberalism,* edited by R. Bruce Douglass and David Hollenbach. Cambridge: Cambridge University Press.

Glenn, Norval, and Ruth Hyland. 1967. Religious Preference and Worldly Success: Some Evidence from National Surveys. *American Sociological Review* 32:73–85.

Glenn, Norval. 1982. Interreligious Marriage in the United States: Patterns and Recent Trends. *Journal of Marriage and the Family,* August, 555–66.

Greeley, Andrew M. 1973. *The New Agenda.* Garden City, N.Y.: Doubleday.

———. 1977. *The American Catholic: A Social Portrait.* New York: Basic Books.

———. 1979. *Crisis in the Church.* Chicago: The Thomas More Association.

———. 1989. Protestant and Catholic: Is the Analogical Imagination Extinct? *American Sociological Review* 54:485–502.

———. 1990. *The Catholic Myth.* New York: Scribner's.

———. 1996. *Catholic Schools in a Declining Church.* Kansas City, Mo.: Sheed & Ward.

———. 1997. Polarized Catholics? Don't Believe Your Mail! *America,* 22 February, 11–15.

———. 1999. Just the Facts Man, *Commonweal,* 17 December, 14–15.

Greene, Dana. 1998. *The Living of Maisie Ward.* Notre Dame, Ind.: University of Notre Dame Press.

Gremillion, Joseph, and Jim Castelli. 1987. *The Emerging Parish.* San Francisco: Harper and Row.

Hadaway, C. Kirk, Penny Long Marler, and Mark Chaves. 1993. What the Polls Don't Show: A Closer Look at U.S. Church Attendance. *American Sociological Review* 58:741–52.

Hall, Douglas T., and Benjamin Schneider. 1973. *Organizational Climates and Careers: The Work Lives of Priests.* New York: Seminar Press.

Herberg, Will. 1960. Protestant–Catholic–Jew. Garden City, N.Y.: Doubleday.

Hockstader, Lee. 2000. 'Selling' Jewishness: Program Flies Youths to Israel. *Washington Post,* 17 January, A1, A19.

Hoge, Dean R. 1976. *Division in the Protestant House.* Philadelphia: Westminster Press.

———. 1987. *The Future of Catholic Leadership: Responses to the Priest Shortage.* Kansas City, Mo.: Sheed & Ward.

———. 1999. Catholic Generational Differences. *America,* 2 October, 14–20.

Hoge, Dean R., Benton Johnson, and Donald A. Luidens. 1994. *Vanishing Boundaries: The Religion of Mainline Protestant Baby Boomers.* Louisville, Ky.: Westminster/John Knox Press.

Hoge, Dean R., William D. Dinges, Mary Johnson, and Juan L. Gonzales. 2001. *Young Adult Catholics: Religion in the Culture of Choice.* Notre Dame, Ind.: University of Notre Dame Press.

Hoge, Dean R., Charles Zech, Patrick McNamara, and Michael J. Donahue. 1996. *Money Matters: Personal Giving in American Churches.* Louisville, Ky.: Westminster John Knox Press.

Hogg, Michael A. 1992. *The Social Psychology of Group Cohesiveness.* New York: New York University Press.

Hogg, Michael A., and Dominic Abrams. 1988. *Social Identifications.* London: Routledge.

Howard, Elaine. 1999. Responding to Modernization: Catholic Women Leading in the Local Congregation. Paper presented at the annual meeting of the American Sociological Association, Chicago.

Hug, James. 1999. *Center Focus: News from the Center of Concern.* Washington, D.C., June–July, 2.

Hunter, James D., and Kimon Sargeant. 1998. The Religious Roots of the Culture Wars:

How Competing Moral Visions Fuel Cultural Conflict. In *The Tribal Basis of American Life*, edited by Murray Friedman. New York: Praeger.

John Paul II, Pope. 1999. *Ecclesia in America*. Washington, D.C.: United States Catholic Conference.

Johnson, Robert A. 1987. *Religious Associative Marriage in the United States*. New York: Academic Press.

Kaiser, Robert Blair. 1985. *The Politics of Sex and Religion*. Kansas City, Mo.: Leaven Press.

Kalmijn, Matthijs. 1991. Shifting Boundaries: Trends in Religious and Educational Homogamy. *American Sociological Review* 56:786–800.

Kelly, James R. 1979. The Spirit of Ecumenism: How Wide, How Deep, How Mindful of Truth? *Review of Religious Research* 20:180–94.

———. 1990. Spirals Not Cycles: Toward an Analytic Approach to the Sources and Stages of Ecumenism. *Review of Religious Research* 32:5–15

Kennedy, Eugene. 1988. *Tomorrow's Catholics, Yesterday's Church*. San Francisco: Harper and Row.

Kennedy, Eugene, and Victor Heckler. 1972. *The Catholic Priest in the United States: Psychological Investigations*. Washington, D.C.: United States Catholic Conference.

Kerbo, Harold R. 1999. *Social Stratification and Inequality*. New York: McGraw–Hill.

Kosmin, Barry A., and Seymour P. Lachman. 1993. *One Nation Under God*. New York: Harmony Books.

Lazerwitz, Bernard. 1961. Some Factors Associated with Variation in Church Attendance. *Social Forces* 39:301–09.

Lee, Bernard, and William D'Antonio. 2000. *The Catholic Experience of Small Christian Communities*. New York: Paulist Press.

Leege, David C., and Paul D. Mueller. 2000. American Catholics at the Catholic Moment. Paper presented at the annual meeting of the American Political Science Association, 1 September, in Washington, D.C.

Lenski, Gerhard. 1961. *The Religious Factor*. Garden City, N.Y.: Doubleday.

Lockwood, Robert P., ed. 2000. *Anti-Catholicism in American Culture*. Huntington, Ind.: Our Sunday Visitor.

Mannion, Msgr. Francis. 2000. How is Christ 'Present' in the Eucharist? *Our Sunday Visitor*, 21 May, 20.

Martin, James. 2000. The Last Acceptable Prejudice? *America*, 25 March, 8–16.

McClory, Robert. 1995. *Turning Point*. New York: Crossroad.

———. 2000. Bishops Ponder New Study of Priest Shortage. *National Catholic Reporter*, 3 June.

McCutcheon, Alan. 1988. Denominations and Religious Intermarriage: Trends among White Americans in the Twentieth Century. *Review of Religious Research* 29:213–27.

McGuire, Rt. Rev. Monsignor Michael A. 1961. *Baltimore Catechism, No. 1*. Revised edition, New York: Benzinger Brothers.

McNamara, Patrick H. 1992. *Conscience First, Tradition Second*. Albany, N.Y.: SUNY Press.

Mitchell, Nathan. 1998. *Real Presence: The Word of Eucharist*. Chicago: Liturgy Training Publications.

Moore, Edmund. 1956. *A Catholic Runs for President*. New York: Ronald Press.

Morris, Charles R. 1997. *American Catholic*. New York: Times Books.

Murnion, Philip. 1992. *New Parish Ministers: Laity and Religious on Parish Staffs.* New York: National Pastoral Life Center.

Murnion, Philip, and David DeLambo. 1999. *Parishes and Parish Ministries.* New York: National Pastoral Life Center.

Murray, John Courtney. 1960. *We Hold These Truths: Catholic Reflections on the American Proposition.* New York: Sheed and Ward.

National Catholic Reporter. 1967. *The Birth Control Debate.* Kansas City, Mo.: NCR Publishing Co.

National Opinion Research Center. 1972. *The Catholic Priest in the United States: Sociological Investigations.* Andrew M. Greeley and Richard A. Schoenherr, co-investigators. Washington, D.C.: U.S. Catholic Conference.

Network Connection, newsletter of NETWORK, a National Catholic Social Justice Lobby, Washington, D.C., January–February 1999, 2.

Newman, William M., and Peter Halvorson. 2000. *Atlas of American Religion: The Denominational Era, 1776–1990.* Walnut Creek, Calif.: AltaMira Press.

Obituary: William Simon. 2000. *Washington Post,* 4 June, C6.

O'Meara, Mary Jane Frances Carolina, Jeffrey Allen Joseph Stone, Maureen Anne Teresa Kelly, and Richard Glen Michael Davis. 1985. *Growing Up Catholic.* Garden City, N.Y.: Doubleday.

Official Catholic Directory. 1998. Annual eds. New Providence, N.J.: P. J. Kenedy.

Osting, Richard N. 2000. Catholicism Struggles with 'Enormous' Priest Shortage. *Associated Press,* 18 June.

Paul VI, Pope. 1968. *Humanae Vitae.* Vatican City. July.

Phillips, Kevin. 1990. *The Politics of the Rich and Poor.* New York: Random House.

The Poor Have Real Problems that Government Must Address. 1998. *Public Perspective,* February–March, 34.

Putnam, Robert. 2000. *Bowling Alone.* New York: Simon and Schuster.

Quinn, Archbishop John. 1999. *Reform of the Papacy.* New York: Crossroad.

Rice, Nick. 1997. Will the Diaconate Become Parochialized? *Origins* 26:746–49.

Roof, Wade Clark, and William McKinney. 1987. *American Mainline Religion.* New Brunswick, N.J.: Rutgers University Press.

Rosenberg, Morris. 1979. *Conceiving the Self.* New York: Basic Books.

Sander, William. 1993. Catholicism and Intermarriage in the United States. *Journal of Marriage and the Family* 55:1037–41.

———. 2000. The Allocation of Time to Religion. Unpublished paper.

Schallert, Eugene J., and Jacqueline M. Kelley. 1970. Some Factors Associated with Voluntary Withdrawal From the Catholic Priesthood. *Lumen Vitae* 25:425–60.

Schemo, Diana Jean, with Marjorie Conne. 1999. In Poll, New York Catholics Call Poverty a Top Concern. *New York Times,* 18 December.

Schoenherr, Richard A., and Andrew M. Greeley. 1974. Role Commitment Processes and the American Catholic Priesthood. *American Sociological Review* 39:407–26.

Schoenherr, Richard A., and Annemette Sorensen. 1982. Social Change in Religious Organizations: Consequences of Clergy Decline in the U.S. Catholic Church. *Sociological Analysis* 43: 23–52.

Schoenherr, Richard A., and Lawrence A. Young. 1993. *Full Pews and Empty Altars: Demographics of the Priest Shortage in United States Catholic Dioceses.* Madison: The University of Wisconsin Press.

Seidler, John. 1974. Priest Resignations, Relocations and Passivity. *National Catholic Reporter* 10 (21 May): 7, 14.

———. 1979. Priest Resignations in a Lazy Monopoly. *American Sociological Review* 44:763–83.

Seidler, John, and Katherine Meyer. 1989. *Conflict and Change in the Catholic Church.* New Brunswick, N.J.: Rutgers University Press.

Shaughnessy, Gerald. [1925] 1969. *Has the Immigrant Kept the Faith?* New York: Arno Press and the *New York Times.*

Shields, Mark. 1999. Choosing the Chaplain: A House Divided. *The Washington Post,* 1 December, A43.

Smith, Christian. 1998. *American Evangelicalism: Embattled and Thriving.* Chicago: University of Chicago Press.

Stark, Rodney, and Charles Y. Glock. 1968. *American Piety: The Nature of Religious Commitment.* Berkeley: University of California Press.

Statistical Abstracts of the United States. 1999. Washington, D.C.: U.S. Department of Commerce.

Steinberg, Stephen. 1974. *The Academic Melting Pot.* New York: McGraw–Hill.

Steinfels, Peter. 1994. Future of Faith Worries Catholic Leaders. *New York Times,* 1 June, A1, B8.

Stryker, Sheldon. 1991. Identity Theory. In *Encyclopedia of Sociology,* Vol. 2, edited by Edgar F. Borgatta and Marie L. Borgatta, New York: Macmillan.

Stryker, Sheldon, and Richard T. Serpe. 1994. Identity Salience and Psychological Centrality: Equivalent, Overlapping, or Complementary Concepts? *Social Psychological Quarterly* 57:16–35.

Taylor, Robert J., Linda M. Chatters, Rukmaile Jayakody, and Jeffrey S. Levin. 1996. Black and White Differences in Religious Participation: A Multisample Comparison. *Journal for the Scientific Study of Religion* 35:403–10.

The Catholic Moment. 1997. N.Y. Surveys Uncover Confusion on Communion, 17 August, 15.

———. 1995. Sociologist Raises Concerns about Mass Attendance Studies, 12 February, 4.

Thorman, Donald. 1962. *The Emerging Layman.* Kansas City, Mo.: Sheed & Ward.

Wallace, Ruth. 1992. *They Call Her Pastor.* Albany, N.Y.: State University of New York Press.

Weaver, Mary Jo. 1999. *What's Left? Liberal American Catholics.* Bloomington, Ind.: Indiana University Press.

Weaver, Mary Jo, and R. Scott Appleby. 1995. *Being Right: Conservative Catholics in America.* Bloomington, Ind.: Indiana University Press.

White, John, and William D'Antonio. 1997. The Catholic Vote in Election '96. *Public Perspective* 8:45–48.

Wilensky, Harold L. 1964. The Professionalization of Everyone? *American Journal of Sociology* 70:137–58.

Wilkes, Paul. 2001. *Excellent Catholic Parishes.* Mahwah, N.J.: Paulist Press.

Wills, Garry. 2000. *Papal Sin: Structures of Deceit.* New York: Doubleday.

Wittberg, Patricia. 1996. *Pathways to Re-Creating Religious Communities.* New York: Paulist Press.

Wright, Charles R., and Herbert H. Hyman. 1958. Voluntary Association Memberships of

American Adults: Evidence from National Sample Surveys. *American Sociological Review* 23:284–94.

Wuthnow, Robert. 1994. *Sharing the Journey*. New York: Free Press.

Young, Lawrence. 1998. Assessing and Updating the Schoenherr–Young Projections of Clergy Decline in the United States Roman Catholic Church. *Sociology of Religion* 59:7–23.

Zaleski, Peter A., and Charles E. Zech. 1994. Economic and Attitudinal Factors in Catholic and Protestant Giving. *Review of Religious Research* 36:197–206.

Index

About the Authors

William V. D'Antonio (Ph.D., Michigan State University, 1958) is a visiting research professor in the Department of Sociology at the Catholic University of America. His interests and writings include religion, ethnicity, politics, and the family. He is the coauthor of six books and coeditor of four and was executive officer of the American Sociological Association from 1982 to 1991. He has served as editor of the ASA journal *Contemporary Sociology,* and is professor emeritus at the University of Connecticut. He has been president of the Society for the Scientific Study of Religion, the Association for the Sociology of Religion, the International Institute of Sociology, and the District of Columbia Sociological Society.

James D. Davidson (Ph.D., University of Notre Dame, 1969) is professor of sociology at Purdue University. He specializes in the sociology of religion, particularly studies of American Catholicism. He is coauthor of *The Search for Common Ground,* which received the 1998 Research Award from the National Conference of Catechetical Leadership. He also writes a syndicated column called "Research for the Church" for diocesan newspapers. He has been president of the Religious Research Association and the North Central Sociological Association, editor of the *Review of Religious Research,* and executive officer of the Society for the Scientific Study of Religion.

Dean R. Hoge (Ph.D., Harvard University, 1970) is professor of sociology and director of the Life Cycle Institute at the Catholic University of America. He served as assistant professor at Princeton Theological Seminary for five years. In 1974 he came to the Catholic University of America, where he has taught ever since. His principal books are *Converts, Dropouts, and Returnees: A*

Study of Change Among Catholics (1981); *The Future of Catholic Leadership: Responses to the Priest Shortage* (1987); *Vanishing Boundaries: The Religion of Protestant Baby Boomers* (coauthored with Benton Johnson and Donald Luidens, 1994), which won the 1994 Distinguished Book Award from the Society for the Scientific Study of Religion; and *Money Matters: Personal Giving to American Churches* (coauthored with Charles Zech, Patrick McNamara, and Michael Donahue, 1996).

Katherine Meyer (Ph.D., University of North Carolina at Chapel Hill, 1974) is a professor in the Department of Sociology at the Ohio State University and has done extensive work on change in the American Catholic Church. In addition to numerous articles, Meyer (with John Seidler) analyzed the conflict surrounding Vatican II in *Conflict and Change in the Catholic Church* (1989). Meyer also has written extensively on the relationship between Islam and democracy in the Middle East and on the U.S. farm crisis, incorporating the association between religion and mental health. She has served as editor of the monograph series for the Society for the Scientific Study of Religion and is treasurer of the organization. She has been secretary–treasurer of the Sociology of Religion section of the American Sociological Association, and is a member of the councils of both the SSSR and the ASA Sociology of Religion section.